What would Jesus say to...?

Steve Ayers & Jason Lane

What would Jesus say to...?

Inter-Varsity Press

INTER-VARSITY PRESS
38 De Montfort Street, Leicester LE1 7GP, England

© Steve Ayers and Jason Lane, 1999

Steve Ayers and Jason Lane have asserted their right under the Copyright, Designs and Patents Act, 1988, to be identified as Authors of this work.

All rights reserved. No part of this publication may be reproduced, stored in a retrieval system, or transmitted, in any form or by any means, electronic, mechanical, photocopying, recording or otherwise, without the prior permission of the publisher or the Copyright Licensing Agency.

Unless otherwise stated, Scripture quotations in this publication are from the Holy Bible, New International Version. Copyright © 1973, 1978, 1984 by International Bible Society. Used by permission of Hodder & Stoughton, a member of the Hodder Headline Group. All rights reserved. 'NIV' is a registered trademark of International Bible Society. UK trademark number 1448790.

First published 1999

British Library Cataloguing in Publication Data
A catalogue record for this book is available from the British Library.

ISBN 0–85111–251–X

Set in Garamond
Typeset in Great Britain
Printed and bound in Great Britain by
Caledonian International Book Manufacturing Ltd, Glasgow

Inter-Varsity Press is the book-publishing division of the Universities and Colleges Christian Fellowship (formerly the Inter-Varsity Fellowship), a student movement linking Christian Unions in universities and colleges throughout Great Britain, and a member movement of the International Fellowship of Evangelical Students. For more information about local and national activities write to UCCF, 38 De Montfort Street, Leicester LE1 7GP.

Contents

Introduction 7
1. Oasis 10
2. Prince Charles 22
3. Bridget Jones 35
4. George Michael 49
5. Geri Halliwell 61
6. Richard Branson 72
7. Steven Spielberg 84
8. Glenn Hoddle 95
9. Mulder and Scully 109
10. Ben Elton 121
11. Billy Graham 131
12. You 143

Introduction

An elderly woman walks out of church. Saddened, she shakes her head and begins to mutter away. She's just witnessed something suspiciously modern at her church service and didn't appreciate it one little bit. In her despair she turns to her companion and declares, 'I don't know, it's enough to make Jesus turn in his grave!'

We've written this book firm in our conviction that Jesus is still alive, having risen from the grave he was buried in. You may or may not share that belief. But each time you write the date on a cheque or fill in a form, the date measures the time since Jesus Christ walked the earth. You may just have noticed the fuss about the millennium, his 2,000th birthday party. It's estimated that a third of the earth's population claim to follow him today. One thing's for certain, you can't deny that Jesus has had a tremendous impact on the planet.

You only have to read one of the four accounts of Jesus' life to see that he was remarkable. The best-selling biographies record the words and deeds of an amazing man. Eyewitness reports of Jesus' life record him healing the sick, raising the dead, and speaking the most profound words imaginable.

We believe that Jesus still has plenty to say. We began to wonder what he'd say about the world that we find ourselves in today. In the twenty-first century, what would Jesus say to the people who make the world's news bulletins on a regular basis? What would Jesus say to Prince Charles? Or to Richard Branson? What would he say to the people that we find ourselves discussing with our friends, people like Geri Halliwell or Glenn Hoddle?

Some of our answers might surprise you, shock you even. But Jesus was in the business of surprising people when he first visited the planet; we're sure that it'd be the same today.

The last thing that we would want to do is put words into Jesus' mouth, so in most chapters of the book we've looked at the way that Jesus spoke with people 2,000 years ago. Sometimes we've looked at other parts of the Bible. If you have your doubts, go back to the stories of Jesus' life, and read them for yourself. Again, prepare to be surprised.

Finally, we have to own up to the fact that this business of 'What would Jesus say to … ?' isn't an original idea. We read and thoroughly enjoyed Lee Strobels' excellent book, which looked at what Jesus would say to a variety of American personalities. That book inspired us to do something similar from a British viewpoint.

So, what if Jesus was to bump into one or two of these celebrities? What would he have to say? To start with, suppose he was at a party and bumped into Liam and Noel Gallagher. (We're sure that he would be at a party; after all it was one of the things that people criticized him for.) What would Jesus have to say to Oasis?

1. What would Jesus say to Oasis?

Football was what they wanted to do if they didn't make it in rock and roll. April 1996 saw them play at Maine Road, the home of their footballing heroes, Manchester City. The stadium was packed. Demand for tickets was so high that the fans totally obscured any view of the hallowed turf. This was an extraordinary homecoming, not of football champions, but of Oasis.

That was one of four record-breaking concerts, two nights at Maine Road, two at Earl's Court. At Knebworth, on two consecutive nights they played to 125,000 fans.

Their third album, *Be Here Now*, went double-platinum in the UK after three days. It became the fastest-selling album ever by a margin of almost two to one.[1]

Always wanting to play live, they gigged consistently until March 1998, playing an exhausting

361 concerts.[2] Their world tour ended in Mexico City with a bang, when Noel's stage amplifier went up in smoke. Some say Oasis went with it.

Since then all's been quieter on the Oasis front. Noel has made occasional on-stage appearances with his favourite bands and another collaboration with the Chemical Brothers. *Masterplan*, a collection of tracks from their CD singles, was released to good critical reviews, and the new album has been recorded in France for release in the first half of 2000.

Quieter, that is, until both Bonehead and Guigsey quit the band. Both were Oasis originals, and their departures again fuelled speculation that Oasis's condition was terminal. Unsurprisingly, Liam and Noel denied everything.

Oasis rose Phoenix-like from the ashes of a band called Rain. They exploded on to the scene and seemed to be unstoppable. For months we couldn't read a newspaper or music magazine without an Oasis headline or photograph. Something about Oasis got under people's skin.

Paul, the older Gallagher brother, accounts for the massive appeal of Oasis by virtue of their message.

'All their songs have universal themes – being free, being positive, making things happen. That's their view of the way life is. Opportunities don't come every day, so when they do, seize them. That's why those ordinary working-class kids in Britain love them, too.'[3] 'Oasis brings hope. Hope to a generation … An impetus to have a dream, chase it and catch it.'[4]

Noel would agree: '… none of us ever expected it

could have been as huge as this. But I think a lot of what we've achieved has come about because we've caught the spirit of what was missing in a lot of people's lives.'[5]

Oasis are the underdogs made good. Theirs is a story of survival and success against the odds. Success fuelled by unquenchable self-belief. They claim to have once played a gig for an audience of nil, even doing an encore. Their analysis: 'It didn't matter, we were brilliant.'[6]

An encounter between Jesus and Oasis might seem like a bit of a mismatch. 'Gentle Jesus Meek and Mild' meets the 'Rock and Roll Rebels from Burnage.' But if Liam and Noel could be persuaded to talk with Jesus, I think they'd be surprised by what he'd say.

Liam and Noel are not fans of the religious. A snapshot of their thinking appeared on the cover of their single 'D'Ya Know What I Mean?' On the front, the band are facing the camera. Behind them there's a crowd of people, all facing left and looking up. The reverse side of the CD cover reveals what they're looking at. A fiery looking man is leaning out of a first-floor window waving a big black book, pointing and screaming at the crowd. He looks like a preacher. Oasis look away.

Liam summed up his attitude in an interview with *GQ* magazine: 'I don't believe in religion basically. I was brought up going to church and after circumstances in my life changed, I thought **** 'em all.'[7]

The truth is that their experience of church and religion was boring. It made no connection with real life, the everyday struggles of getting by. Like so many others, they walked out and won't be coming back.

Jesus might start by saying: 'I'm not what you think.'

If Liam and Noel would talk with Jesus, they'd be amazed how much they had in common. No doubt the brothers would expect him to be like the man on the CD sleeve – angry and judgmental. I think they'd be amazed to hear Jesus say, 'I agree with you. I don't believe in religion either. Avoid it at all costs. Religion is lethal.'

That may surprise you too. But part of Jesus' message was that in order for people to really live, they must lose their religion. Jesus frequently spoke out against the religious leaders of his day and warned others to avoid their lifeless orthodoxy, risking his life as he did. On one occasion he met a top-ranking religious leader who had come under the cover of night to talk to him. Jesus' reply demolished his pretensions. This religious high-flier was told that if he really wanted to connect with God (something he thought was sewn up by his religious devotion), he'd have to start his life all over again.[8] The point was simple. Religion doesn't work. So lose it.

Hardly subtle and hardly the contemporary image of Jesus as a pale-faced, softly spoken, lamb-carrying wimp who hovers six inches above the ground! But that's the point. Many modern understandings of Jesus bear no resemblance to the original. The real Jesus would definitely agree with Liam and Noel on the pointlessness of religion. Maybe that would get their attention.

And Jesus would get their attention by taking the time to listen. He'd listen to their experiences, opinions, frustrations and their music. And then I can just imagine Jesus asking them a question. A question that very few people would brave asking the likes of Liam Gallagher: 'Behind the image and the attitude I can see you're restless. What is it that you really want?'

Liam and Noel are famous for their 'don't care' attitude, which is epitomized by Liam's on-stage stance and his 'C'mon'. But behind the image are people who have important things they long for. Liam summed it up in a TV interview: 'I just live my life the way I want to live it. I want to have fun ... everyone has their fair share of fun ... you gotta have fun, haven't you?'[9]

Like all of us, Liam and Noel want to be happy, they want to have a good time. Who would disagree with that? And like most of us they have their own idea how to do it. On the single 'Whatever', they sing about being free. Free to do and say what they want. Living without limits. It's the 'do it yourself' guide to happiness and fulfilment. Freedom is the anthem of the decade. Just do it. And millions of us sing along with them. The song, together with the attitude and the lifestyle, tells their watching public where they think they'll find the happiness they crave.

Ironically, it's that same 'live for ever', 'roll with it' attitude that's now being rejected as unreal. The hope they generated is being replaced by cynicism. The Oasis backlash has begun.

To which Jesus would say, 'I know about your search because I know about you. I can help you find what you're looking for.' Then I can just imagine Jesus telling Liam and Noel a story.

The story is of a father and his two sons. The younger son wants to be free to do whatever. He's had enough of the restrictions and responsibilities of living at home. He's through with having to do what his father says. He wants to cut loose and sail away. So he goes to his father and gives him the news that he wishes he was dead. Sure, he didn't put it quite so starkly, but the father knew exactly what he meant. He was saying that he couldn't hang around. If his father insisted on living, could he just have what was due to him now?

'Father, give me my share of the estate.'[10]

This is a scandalous request, and the Jews who heard the story would have been very ready to give the young man what was due to him. And it wouldn't have been his inheritance! Yet amazingly, his dad gives him what he wants.

'So he divided his property between them.'

You can imagine the son running through the gates of the house, heading for the big smoke, punching the air with delight and thinking, 'Free at last!'

And the father's heart breaking.

So the boy heads off and does some severe partying. We're not told what he got up to – we could probably guess – but we are told it was wild![11]

No restrictions, no limits, no-one telling him what to do or when to come in. Life was now entirely his call. He was out of reach of his father's rules, free to do whatever.

God is often seen in the same way that the partying son viewed his father. Not as a DJ, but a killjoy. A force for misery and boredom. Someone who specializes in inventing rules so as to spoil our fun. A party-pooper of cosmic proportions!

Andrew was the first guy I met at university and he thought just that. His experience of church was almost identical to Liam and Noel's. When he found out that I was a Christian he laughed. 'What, "Christian"? Like, no sex?' He thought that God was out to spoil his fun and so he wanted nothing to do with him.

When Oasis sing 'Whatever' we sing with them. The search for freedom and happiness is part of our experience. The search of the son in this story is as relevant today as when Jesus spoke. Everyone searches. We look in different places. But we all look for that something or someone who will set us free and make us complete: the career, the house, the perfect partner, the most intense experience. The fact of the search tells us that we still haven't found what we're looking for.

You might expect Jesus to say that the boy was thoroughly miserable and didn't enjoy himself one bit. After all, he had walked out on his father. But he didn't, because it's not true. In fact it would seem that the son was having a great time. Jesus describes him getting so carried away that he ran clean out of cash. Blowing your inheritance on a party is some feat! But with his head still aching and his ears still ringing, he sets out to find a way of reducing his overdraft and winds up temping as a pig farmer.

There would have been an audible gasp from the listening crowd as Jesus described a Jew getting a job as a pig farmer. The Jews regarded the pig as an unclean animal. This was like a vegetarian working in an abattoir!

Maybe the smell woke him up. Sitting among the pigs, home didn't seem so bad. Dad didn't seem such an ogre. In fact, his father's words of warning as he walked out of the house made sense now. Why hadn't he listened?

Jesus is highlighting a fundamental fact. People need parameters. We're designed to live within certain limits. Travel beyond them and we inevitably lose our bearings. True freedom, Jesus would say, is not freedom to do whatever, but freedom to be who we are meant to be. Limits are a sign of love. Parents protect their children by preventing them wandering into a dangerous place. Boundaries are set not by a God who controls but by a God who cares. God's rules are positive, for our protection and well-being. Going outside them won't always result in disaster and it may sometimes be fun. But it will never give us what we really want – soul satisfaction. The son's bid for freedom was always going to fail, because it contradicted who he was. Ours will too.

Six months after our initial encounter, and now a firm friend, Andrew was back in my room again. He had become a university legend, known for leading the way in the campaign for real parties. This time he wasn't saying that Jesus was out of touch. He was crying. The 'do whatever' definition of freedom that he'd lived by had caught up with him. His latest relationship had failed and he was shattered. No-one had told him that a condom couldn't protect him from a broken heart.

Jesus would say to Liam and Noel, 'Freedom is found in knowing me. It's how you work best. I don't want to restrict you; I want to give you life to the full.[12] More and better than you dreamed of.' And he'd say the same to you.

The boy in Jesus' story decides to return home and seek his father's forgiveness. He figures that he's blown it as a son and will offer his services as a paid servant. You can well imagine him rehearsing his apology as he walks towards the house. How would his father respond? Have the locks been changed? After all that's happened, will he still want to know?

The locks haven't been changed; in fact the door's wide open. Dad's been waiting, looking, longing for the return of the son who had wished him dead. So when the boy appears on the horizon, Dad forgets social etiquette and sprints down the road, throws his arms around him, and utters two words which would have melted the heart of the runaway – 'my son'.

The father takes his lost son home, and gives him the best of what he has – new clothes and new shoes, a huge party with fine food, and best of all, he gives his son a ring to wear – the sign of being part of the family.

Jesus would say to Liam and Noel, 'That's how I

feel about you. You can know real freedom because you can know me. The father in the story is a picture of how I feel about you. I love you and will gladly welcome you home.'

This may be appealing. Who wouldn't want to find the relationship for which they were made? But at the same time, I think Liam and Noel would find Jesus' offer hard to believe. Their experience of a father has not been of someone who loved them unconditionally and gave them another chance when they messed up. It's been quite the opposite.

The boys witnessed their mother being mistreated and humiliated and were themselves harshly and sometimes violently treated. Their father made them work for him, usually without pay, and had a fierce temper which made the boys fear his every move. Their brother Paul describes their father as 'a walking persecution'.[13]

Perhaps the results of that experience were seen in a televised interview with Liam, where we were given a rare glimpse of the man in the iron attitude: 'Everyone gets told they're worthless, don't they? No-one gives you a chance in this world. You've always got some **** putting you down, haven't you?'[14]

Jesus would say, 'I will give you the chance you've always wanted. Come to me and I will welcome you home. You've broken my heart by shouting, "I wish you were dead" and living as if I was. But if you'll turn around and come home I'll welcome you back.'

Liam and Noel are not known for their humility. I think Jesus might finish the conversation by reminding them that if they want real freedom and all that comes with it, they will have to make a change.

First, Jesus would say, 'You need to admit you're lost.'

One of the great difficulties with being lost is that you don't always realize it. I once drove around a city in Germany for several hours convinced I was nearly in Calais. All I had done was drive around the same ring road!

Jesus provides the reality check. Whether we know it or not, whether we feel it or not, we are lost. Like the son in the story, finding the right way requires that we admit we're down a blind alley. That we've chased an impossible dream. Impossible because the escape to 'freedom' contradicts who we are.

Second, Jesus would say, 'Liam, Noel, you need to take responsibility. Despite your experiences of church and the pain your father caused, you still have real choices to make about me.'

Like the father in the story, God doesn't force anyone's hand. He gives real people real choices because with them comes the possibility of real freedom. Taking responsibility for getting up and walking out was the best thing the son could do, because it left him just one short journey from home. A journey that only he could make.

'Liam, Noel, you can come home any time. No recriminations. You can have what you've always wanted. Freedom can be a reality,' Jesus would say. 'It's found in knowing me. The answer is right here, right now.'

This is nothing to do with restrictive religion. Who would want that? On the other hand, who wouldn't want to live by principles that are designed to maximize our pleasure and bring soul-satisfaction, for us and others? Real freedom is the ability to live like that. Rule-bound religion is the opposite and puts people off searching for the real thing. That's why Jesus was so down on religion. So, if you're thinking that Jesus and religion are one and the same, why not take another look?

Oh, and don't forget. Whatever it is, religion, rock and roll or football, it won't do the job. You need to lose your religion, find freedom and live for ever.

2. What would Jesus say to Prince Charles?

On 14 November 1948, naval guns fired and church bells rang, announcing the birth of one Charles Philip Arthur George. Clearly this was no ordinary Charles Philip Arthur George! This was the child who would become His Royal Highness Prince Charles Philip Arthur George, Prince of Wales and Earl of Chester, Duke of Cornwall, Duke of Rothesay, Earl of Carrick, Lord of the Isles and Baron of Renfrew, Prince and Great Stewart of Scotland.

Charles was born the boy who would be king. Royal life is undoubtedly unique – brought up in Buckingham Palace, life under the spotlight and round-the-clock high security. He even had a detective responsible for laundry while he was at university, to protect the royal underpants from souvenir hunters! He would always have been a figure of keen interest to the media, but his marriage to and subsequent divorce from Princess Diana made him an even greater focus of attention.

It hasn't all been easy by any means. He was often home alone, while his parents were on royal duties. His relationship with his father appears to have been particularly difficult, as Prince Philip tried to prepare his son for the rigours of public life.

At school, Charles struggled to make friends: 'I'm not a gregarious person so I've always had a horror of gangs ... I have always preferred my own company or just a one to one.'[1] The heir to the throne did not escape the attention of the playground bully, and, unfortunately for Charles, doing over the future king of England was seen as a worthwhile diversion, especially on the rugby pitch.

Surprisingly for some, the prince suffered from chronically low self-esteem, something that he struggled with through school and beyond. In a letter to his much-loved uncle, Lord Mountbatten, written while he was serving in the Royal Navy, he wrote: ' ... I'm afraid I tend to suffer from bouts of hopeless depression because I feel I'm never going to cope ... I find I appear even more useless than usual.'[2]

For the future king of England, with the wealth and status that brings, Charles is a man still unsure of himself. In a Cambridge University speech he described his difficulty: 'My great problem in life is that I do not really know what my role in life is. At the moment I do not have one. But somehow I must find one.'[3] Because fifty years later he is still king in waiting, Charles has undergone one of the longest apprenticeships in history. Yet no-one can accuse Prince Charles of being inactive. In his search for a role he has established a long list of associations and interests – from his work with young people through the Prince's Trust (were you at the Party in the Park?) to his concern for all things architectural and environmental. In the latter he was ahead of the game in his support for organic farming, farming this way himself while the majority looked on and laughed. He has attracted admiration and dismay in equal measure, when speaking out about matters close to his heart, from architecture to genetically modified foods.

The infamous *Panorama* interview with Charles highlighted his satisfaction with his organic farm in Highgrove, describing it as 'a haven of meaning'. The turn of phrase is extremely telling. Charles is a man who is not quite at ease with himself or the world, someone who is looking for something. Beneath his involvements and interests lies a deeply spiritual man. In fact, his interest in such things as organic farming, architecture and healing are all a result of wanting to acknowledge the spiritual in life.

He despairs of the way that so many in the West have put their trust in scientific materialism. 'Religion and science have become separated, and science has attempted to separate the natural world from God.'[4] Thus he believes that if we segregate the sacred from the everyday, and 'technology becomes a "virtual reality" God; the arbiter of virtual reality ethics',[5] then we become impoverished. His organic farming and interest in architecture are two examples of his desire to get back to the sacred in the everyday.

This theme of a search for the sacred is something that started early in Charles's life. In school the prince sought spiritual peace and was dismayed to find that the pupils' place of worship did not aid him in his quest. He described it as 'hopeless, there's no atmosphere of the mysterious that a church gives one ...'[6]

While he may not have been very impressed, his eager spiritual exploration was noticed by more than one member of the clergy. In Cambridge, where Prince Charles became the first royal to obtain a degree, the Dean of Chapel at Trinity College was excited: 'I always thought he was a deep person, that he wasn't taken in by the surfaces of life. He had an interest in the deeper things of life, in the source of life, an openness of mind, a readiness to evaluate ideas, not taking things off the peg but thinking them out for himself ... It may sound absurd but I always thought he had the making of a saint when he was young ...'[7]

What would Jesus think? I'm sure he'd be excited too. Jesus always celebrated people's spiritual enquiry. He valued the seeker and the seeking process and I think he would want Prince Charles to know that. He would also want Charles to know that seeking for God can be a difficult and uncomfortable thing to do, but that the rewards are worth it. I think Jesus would encourage Charles by reminding him that those who genuinely search for the truth would find it: 'Ask and it will be given to you; seek and you will find; knock and the door will be opened to you. For everyone who asks receives, he who seeks finds; and to him who knocks, the door will be opened.'[8]

I'm sure that Charles is engaged in a genuine search for spiritual truth. Charles has thought long and hard, fuelled by the belief 'that in each of us there is a distant echo of the sense of the sacred, but that the majority of us are terrified to admit its existence for fear of ridicule or abuse'.[9] Distressed by the lack of any great sense of sacred values within much of the Christian tradition, his search has been a wide one. Charles's search has taken him to different times, places and people far beyond the boundaries of Christian orthodoxy, although on his website he is happy to describe himself as a 'practising Anglican'.

While still at Cambridge, he was fascinated by accounts of psychic goings on and looked for a while into the realm of parapsychology. Later he was attracted by the writings of the mystic and explorer, Laurens van der Post. They began a dialogue, in which van der Post encouraged the prince to explore the 'inward way', which it was suggested should include a seven-week trip to the Kalahari Desert. While the prince was keen, the Foreign Office was not!

Eventually, Prince Charles joined van der Post in Kenya, on a five-day exploration of the 'natural and inner worlds'. He continued to look East, reading about Hinduism and Buddhism and developing a belief in reincarnation. During this time he received a book from a Buddhist who told of her mission to convert him to an understanding of the role of the Masters. That book, *The Path of the Masters*, changed

Charles's lifestyle and beliefs. Key to this was the conclusion that religious experience should be seen as 'free of creed and dogma but compatible with all faiths'.[10]

His religious search, which started in earnest in the 1970s, has never ended. More recently he has been extolling the virtues of aspects of Islamic culture. His disenchantment with the disunity of the Christian community and his belief that the major religions of the world were saying much the same thing have led to his conviction that 'salvation springs less from religion than from faith'.[11]

Jesus would agree with this, at least in part. Salvation has nothing to do with religion and everything to do with faith. As Charles himself noted in Radio 4's 'Thought for the Day', 'the Latin origin of the word "religion" means "to bind"'.[12] Many people have been bound up in religion but have not practised faith. Only faith can save. The key question in all this, of course, is the object of that faith. What or who is that faith in?

For Charles it seems that the specific faith that is practised is less important than getting in touch with the sacred. Indeed, he urges that the West turn to Islamic teachers in order to rediscover our spiritual nature: 'But in the West, in turn, we need to be taught by Islamic teachers how to learn once again with our hearts, as well as our heads. I hope we shall not ignore the opportunity this gives us to rediscover the spiritual underpinning of our entire existence.'[13]

Charles has a problem. He believes that a religious faith, a sense of the sacred, is a very important thing.

He also appears to believe that having a faith is more important than what that faith is. You may not see that as a problem; it probably isn't for a great number of people. But Charles's position in society makes it a particularly difficult position to maintain.

The difficulty comes because Charles is due to inherit yet another title when he becomes king, namely Supreme Governor of the Church of England. This requires him to become Defender of the (Christian) Faith. So his views on the validity of all religions have, unsurprisingly, brought him into conflict with sections of the established church, which, in common with some other groups, wishes the prince would be less vocal in advocating the merits of other religious faiths.

In June 1994 Charles went public on his religious views and his role as 'Defender of the Faith', during a TV documentary: 'I personally would rather see it as Defender of faith, not the Faith, because it [Defender of the Faith] means just one particular interpretation of the Faith, which I think is sometimes something that causes a great deal of problem. People have fought each other to the death over these things, which seems to me to be a peculiar waste of people's energy when we're all actually aiming for the same ultimate goal, I think.'[14]

In a conversation with Charles about spiritual reality, I think Jesus would zero in on this. I'm sure Jesus would express the same dismay about the disunity and petty wrangling of the church. I'm certain that Jesus, like Charles, would deplore fighting to the death over religious belief. That was never any part of Christ's manifesto. Charles is to be applauded for his repeated desire that people of different faiths talk to each other and practise tolerance towards each other. The alternative is awful. As Charles highlighted at the memorial service for King Hussein in July 1999, we need to be able 'to respect the followers of other faiths for their piety and moral character, even if we do not accept them theologically'.[15] As a bottom line, other people have the right to disagree with us and live!

But more importantly, Jesus would help Charles with the search of his life. He would offer a unique perspective on his questions and challenge Charles's conclusions. Because these questions of religious truth are timeless, and cut across cultures. Jesus met countless individuals who asked the same questions.

Perhaps Jesus would take Prince Charles back to an encounter he had with one of those people – a woman he met by a well under the searing heat of the midday sun. She was an outcast in her society. No-one fetched water in the hottest part of the day; they chose the cool of morning or evening. But to avoid the scathing comments and daggered looks of her peers, this woman was at the well at the hottest and quietest time of the day.

To her surprise, Jesus is also at the well. Even more amazingly, breaking all the rules and social conventions of his time, Jesus stops and opens the conversation by asking her for a drink. No wonder the woman is astonished. Here's Jesus, a Jew, speaking to a Samaritan, one of a hated minority race. Not only that but he was speaking as a man to a woman. These things didn't tend to happen in this culture. 'The Samaritan woman said to him, "You are a Jew and I am a Samaritan woman. How can you ask me for a drink?" (For Jews do not associate with Samaritans.)'[16]

To compound the shock, Jesus then offers *her* a drink! But it sounds unlike any water she's ever tasted before. He offers her something called 'living water'. Not unnaturally, the woman is completely confused by this and points out that he doesn't even have a bucket. '"Sir," the woman said, "you have nothing to draw with and the well is deep. Where can you get this living water?"'[17]

> Jesus answered, 'Everyone who drinks this water will be thirsty again, but whoever drinks the water I give him will never thirst. Indeed, the water I give him will become in him a spring of water welling up to eternal life.'
>
> The woman said to him, 'Sir, give me this water so I won't get thirsty and have to keep coming here to draw water.'[18]

This is great! Ethnic and gender barriers are falling – a Jewish man is having a conversation with a Samaritan woman; one has offered a gift to the other, who is willing to accept it. And then Jesus tells her to do something that she can't do:

> He told her, 'Go, call your husband and come back.'
>
> 'I have no husband,' she replied.

Jesus said to her, 'You are right when you say you have no husband. The fact is, you have had five husbands, and the man you now have is not your husband. What you have said is quite true.'[19]

This woman has loved and lost five times and now is living with number six. This is why she is treated as an outcast by the rest of the village. A dim view was taken of anyone married more than three times, and as for simply living together – no chance. This is why she's ashamed to collect her water when everyone else does.

Jesus' incredible insight into her circumstances arrests her attention. She concludes that Jesus must be someone special, someone sent from God: "Sir," the woman said, "I can see that you are a prophet."'[20]

It's not every day that you have the chance of a one to one with a prophet! So she makes the most of this unexpected opportunity to ask a troubling question. The same question that has perplexed Prince Charles. You can almost hear the confusion in her voice. What is the right way to worship? Which path to God?

Like Charles, she's searched. She's experienced pain and disappointment. She's been ridiculed for her unorthodox views. She's probably feeling cynical about the whole religious deal, but her need for certainty and hope drives her on.

'Our fathers worshipped on this mountain, but you Jews claim that the place where we must worship is in Jerusalem.'

Jesus declared, 'Believe me, woman, a time is coming when you will worship the Father [God] neither on this mountain nor in Jerusalem. You Samaritans worship what you do not know; we worship what we do know, for salvation is from the Jews. Yet a time is coming and has now come when the true worshippers will worship the Father in spirit and truth, for they are the kind of worshippers the Father seeks.'[21]

Jesus doesn't say all religions are equally valid – that Jews and Samaritans are headed up the same mountain, just by different routes. He says salvation (or rescue) comes from the Jews. Because Jesus, God's rescuer, is a Jew. God has turned up in person to show us what he's like and to light up the way home. Guesswork and debate are redundant. Jesus spells out what true worship – genuine connection with God – looks like. Jesus would want Charles to understand this.

It's often suggested that Jesus wasn't talking about the way to God but about an attitude. Sincere worship is what matters. What you believe is not that important as long as you're sincere. Sincerity is what counts.

A few years ago I travelled to India. I arrived in the middle of the night, not knowing a great deal about the place other than you drove on the right. I'd been told that the driving was somewhat 'creative', so I had got this fact straight in my mind. You can imagine my horror when the woman who'd come to collect me careered off down the left-hand side of the road.

There was I, white-faced (so I was told) and open-mouthed, flying down the highway in the dark, sure I was about to die. When another car passed ours going in the same direction, the driver just looked over, smiled and waved.

I was fast coming to the conclusion that everyone was mad and that I had to get out, when it happened again. And again. And then I got it. I'd got it wrong. In India you drive on the left.

In some situations sincerity doesn't help. My opinion about Indian driving was sincerely held. But it was sincerely wrong. If I'd acted on it, I would have been sincerely dead!

Jesus' concern for Prince Charles, and for us, would be that we base our journey on spiritual reality. That as we seek the answers to our biggest questions of life and identity and God, we look in the right places. Is Jesus trustworthy? Jesus would invite Charles to continue to look carefully at what he said and did. To consider who he could (and couldn't) be.

Lastly, I think Jesus would invite us to ask him the question. To ask him to let us know if he's really there. To risk the possibility of an answer that changes us for ever.

Angie is someone who did just that. She wrote to me describing her search:

> I knew there had to be more. I was carrying all
> this stuff and it was getting me down because I

couldn't shift it. I did what you talked about. I asked him to show me if he was real, if he cared. I began to read the Bible; I talked and asked lots of questions. I even prayed. And now six months later I know. He has shown me and I'm changing.

If you're like Angie or want to be, why not do the same thing? Remember those words that Jesus speaks to anybody searching for the spiritual in their lives, whether royalty or not: 'Ask and it will be given to you; seek and you will find; knock and the door will be opened to you. For everyone who asks receives, he who seeks finds; and to him who knocks, the door will be opened.'

3. What would Jesus say to Bridget Jones?

The Ten Commandments of Bridget Jones

1. Thou shalt never have a boyfriend who wears (out of choice) a V-neck diamond pattern jumper, of the style favoured by Frank Bough.
2. Thou shalt not suffer from unattractiveness hang-up.
3. Thou shalt not live one's life through men.
4. Thou shalt always have a steamed ginger pudding from Marks and Spencer on hand.
5. Thou shalt always have a helpful Tom-like ('so sweetly supportive') friend in your life.
6. When Feng Shui-ing your house, thou shalt not have a rubbish bin in your 'helpful friends' corner.

7. Thou shalt not start relationships with commitment phobics.
8. Thou shalt have a job with potential.
9. Thou shalt remind yourself regularly and often that 'I am a "centred" woman of substance, achieving "the flow" while going with the vibes'.
10. At all costs, thou shalt avoid dying alone, to be discovered half-eaten by an alsatian.

Bridget Jones's Diary is 'miraculously observed' in the opinion of novelist Jilly Cooper,[1] while ringing with the 'unmistakable tone of something that is true to the marrow' and presenting a 'perfect *Zeitgeist* of single females' woes',[2] according to press reviews.

The agonies and ecstasies (mostly agonies) of this thirtysomething, single – but trying hard not to be – woman, produced a rare blockbuster in the book world, Helen Fielding selling over a million copies. Bridget's relational and alcoholic hangovers, her obsession with calories and worrying addiction to Lottery Instants, seem to strike a chord with a lot of people. It's as if someone has read our diaries and decided that it'd be fun to publish them.

Put simply, we identify with Bridget Jones. She shares our anxiety about getting stuck in a dead-end job and left on the shelf. She has a love-hate relationship with relationships. She searches for security and all the time has to endure parental pressure to settle down, and she's honest about how she feels about it.

Some people may think that Jesus would find her

too hot to handle. Too frank, too honest for the sensitivities of a 'religious type'. But I think that her honesty would be one of many things Jesus would appreciate about her. Honesty is a great attribute, especially honesty about yourself. After all, without that kind of self-awareness how can you go about making any changes for the better? Bridget's rigorous self-assessment of her needs and insecurities is perhaps where our greatest identification lies. It's as if, when she looks into the mirror, we see our own reflection looking back.

I think Jesus would appreciate her desire and determined attempts to improve herself – her goal-setting (her diary starts with two whole pages of New Year's resolutions) and her willingness to learn from the past. And I think he'd understand her frustration at not being able to make it work. So I think Jesus may issue her with an invitation. 'You've tried a long list of do's and don'ts. Why don't you try mine now? See if they don't work for you, as they have for millions of people like you.'

They are probably the last things Bridget would consider. Talk of 'do's and don'ts' is often thought of as a euphemism for a boring and fun-free existence – exactly what Bridget is trying to avoid. Or perhaps it brings about images of judgment for the things we've done wrong; images of fire and brimstone being hurled by an obnoxious God at little grey people cowering in a little grey world. Either way, it's not wildly attractive.

But I can imagine Jesus taking Bridget through the Ten Commandments, for instance, explaining how they're written as a guide to life with God and others that is secure, harmonious and fulfilling. That they centre on exactly what she's looking for – satisfying relationships. The tone of the language is sometimes lost in the sound of 'The Ten Commandments'. It sounds harsh and severe and conjures up images of Charlton Heston in the film. But the language of the Bible portrays a loving protector who is urging us not to do certain things for our own good. After getting that straight, Jesus would explain these rules to Bridget. Perhaps he would start with this one: 'You shall not make for yourself an idol in the form of anything in heaven above or on the earth beneath or in the waters below. You shall not bow down to them.'[3]

Talk of idols may sound out of date to you. After all, they're not the kind of things you tend to see when out on a Friday night. Idols were objects of worship and affection, and often the rites and rituals associated with them would dominate a person's life. When seen in that light, as things that dominate a person's life, maybe they're more common than we realize. There are plenty of things that have taken the place of traditional idols. Stop for a moment and think about the things that people trust to bring them peace and meaning, love and hope, identity and security. Those are all things that we long for, and that idols were believed to provide.

Perhaps Bridget has idols too. Her diary points to what they could be. The main thrust of her diary is concerned with her hunt for a partner, that special person who will bring her peace, meaning and security. Someone to take away the loneliness. Here's her diary entry for Friday 13 October: 'Oh God, I'm so lonely. An entire weekend stretching ahead of me with no one to love or have fun with.'[4]

So how to attract that man? Is the answer to lose weight? To be more attractive?

Saturday 22 April
Today is an historic and joyous day. After eighteen years of trying to get down to 8st 7 I have finally achieved it. It is no trick of the scales, but confirmed by jeans. I am thin.[5]

Yet at the same time her experience is of relationships and weight-loss programmes that don't deliver:

Sunday 15 January
Can't believe it. Am stood up. Entire waste of whole day's bloody effort and hydroelectric body-generated power. However, one must not live one's life through men but must be complete in oneself as a woman of substance.[6]

Tuesday 25 April
Now I feel empty and bewildered – as if a rug has been pulled from under my feet. Eighteen years – wasted ... Eighteen years of struggle, sacrifice and endeavour – for what? Eighteen years and the result is 'tired and flat'. I feel like a scientist who discovers that his life's work has been a total mistake.[7]

Dashed hopes and desperate disappointment are common currency. The dream sometimes – more often than we care to admit – morphs into a nightmare.

Jesus would say to Bridget, 'I want to protect you from that. That's why I say, "Don't Do Idols." I know you're looking for security and intimacy. They are vital and wonderful. "Don't Do Idols" is my way of protecting you from the pain and disappointment of a broken promise. You see, pain will always come if you look to people and possessions to give you perfection – if you look for them to give you what only I can.'

That's why 'idols' are to be avoided. They are simply substitutes for God, and poor ones at that. They cannot know as God knows, or love as God loves. Replacing God with anything else – which is a good definition of idolatry – is an exercise in futility.

The Bible – written to tell us about God – contains many descriptions of God's love. Here are just some ways various people describe their experience of it:

> 'You are ... forgiving ... gracious and compassionate, slow to anger and abounding in love.'[8]

> 'I trust in your unfailing love.'[9]

> 'May your unfailing love be my comfort.'[10]

> 'You are forgiving and good, O Lord,

abounding in love to all who call to you."[11]

How about that? I don't know of anything or anyone who loves like that. I don't know of anyone who loves completely all of the time. Do you? There are people who I know love me deeply, but they're not like that. There are people whom I love deeply, but I still disappoint and hurt them.

Idols, even the modern-day sophisticated ones, which live and breathe and love, can't accurately depict or replace God. That's why looking to anything or anyone to love in place of God is as effective as substituting a Marks and Spencer ginger pudding, however well steamed, for a committed friend.

Do you see why God gives us the command about idols? It's to prevent us from settling for second best and to protect us from the inevitable heartache of disappointed hopes. God spells it out because he knows our tendency to get drawn into building life around what often turns out to be a mirage.

A cursory glance at Bridget Jones's diary tells you that she's a hopeless romantic. She still dreams of her knight in shining armour whisking her away and living happily ever after. Whether it's in marriage or outside, that search for someone to share life with is a very attractive proposition for Bridget, as it is for all of us. So next I think Jesus would talk to Bridget about sex. It would certainly get her attention!

If there's one thing people think God is down on, it's sex. You could get the impression that God really doesn't approve of it; that as a major concession he allows it for married couples, but he still isn't that happy about it! But let me assure you, that's far from the God of the Bible. He came up with the idea in the first place! In the Bible's description of the first couple, God tells us what he thinks about sex: 'For this reason a man will leave his father and mother and be united to his wife, and they will become one flesh.'[12] (This is the Bible's poetic language for talking about sex.) That's a great start. God invented sex, and told the first couple to get on with it!

So it follows that what God has to say about sex is for the good of sex and for good sex! The next commandment that Jesus would talk to Bridget about is for precisely that and a lot more besides, and is the core policy in God's pro-sex campaign: 'You shall not commit adultery.'[13]

Bridget isn't married, so it's tempting to think this doesn't apply. But she has seen what happens when this instruction is ignored. Her diary recounts the aftershock of her mother's affair with Julian. She stood helplessly by as her parents' marriage disintegrated and her dad fought to stay afloat under the weight of his wife leaving him for someone else. Her own experience of her boyfriend Daniel's 'hurtful and humiliating' infidelity gave her an insight into the emotional and relational wreckage that follows from not taking this seriously.

> It's no good. When someone leaves you, apart from missing them, apart from the fact that the whole little world you've created together collapses, and that everything you see or do

reminds you of them, the worst is the thought that they've tried you out and, in the end, the whole sum of parts which adds up to you got stamped REJECT by the one you love. How can you not be left with the personal confidence of a passed over British Rail sandwich?[14]

God's instructions for sex include this: 'Only to be used in a suitable and safe environment.' God himself defines that as marriage – where one woman and one man make a life-long, exclusive commitment to each other.

Bridget and her friends rail against men who are 'trying to have sex without any niceness or commitment ...' They don't want to be used and traded in for a newer model, or just used and dumped. Who does? And that's one of the soul-gutting experiences that this guideline avoids.

But there's more. Increased commitment makes for better sex, or, in the words of one *Cosmopolitan* cover, 'Love + Commitment = Mind-blowing Sex!'

That's because sex is more than machinery. It's a God-given means of expressing love, trust, loyalty and partnership. Those things flourish in the context of exclusive commitment and so does sex. Life-long is maximum commitment. Life-long is the safest place to be vulnerable, to be honest and to learn. As the commitment of marriage provides the means for those things to grow, sex gets better too. God wants you to have the best sex life possible! He even tells you how.

If sex is meant only for marriage, it follows it's not

for outside. Remove the firewall of a marriage commitment and the tremendous positive power of sex can turn dangerous and destructive. To be fair (to a fictional character!), Bridget doesn't want just sex. She longs for the intimacy and companionship that a lasting relationship brings. Sex without the relationship leaves her feeling like an object. God's laws offer protection from that. They protect us from being used, from fear of being compared to others and the insecurity that can follow, from disease and destroyed self-esteem. God is not offering better 'safer' sex, but the best, safe sex.

You may be reading this and thinking, 'That really does make sense. I can see how doing it God's way can maximize pleasure and minimize pain, but I haven't lived like that. No-one explained to me the relational risks, and it's too late to turn back the clock.' You may feel, as someone once expressed to me, that 'there are bits of me in every bed and I can never get them back'.

I doubt whether there is anyone, Bridget included, who wouldn't take the opportunity to do some things very differently. I think Jesus would end his conversation with Bridget by helping her see new horizons. Change is an option. A new start is possible. One-time failure, even many-time failure, does not mean the end of the road.

Bridget Jones's Diary begins with a set of New Year's resolutions. The diary ends with a summary of the year that was. She managed to keep just one. Her somewhat ironic conclusion: 'A year of excellent progress.'[15]

It wasn't for the want of trying. She did so much right. She took responsibility, set herself goals and was constantly measuring her progress. She had encouragement in the form of friends and numerous self-help techniques, but frustratingly, she seemed unable to help herself.

I think Jesus would end his exploration of a couple of God's rules for living by saying, 'That's the point, you can't help yourself.' As you've been reading this you may have been thinking, 'These rules are great in theory but not in practice. No-one can keep these. It's just not possible. We're set up for a fall.' And that's the point! It isn't as if I've picked the hardest two of the ten, either.[16] The other commandments aren't any easier:

> You shall not steal.
>
> Do not give false testimony against your neighbour.
>
> Honour your father and mother.
>
> Do not be jealous of anything that belongs to your neighbour.

Do you know anyone who's managed those? I mean really kept them without glossing over that 'raiding' of the biscuit tin or of 'borrowing' of the office stationery? I don't. And I haven't managed to keep them myself either. My performance is poor. My attempts at self-help seem futile. It's not that I don't try, but I can't do it. Not for long, anyway.

God's commandments are for our own good. But they also serve to tell us that we're not good. They point out our failure to measure up to God's standards and highlight the fact that we often don't even manage to reach our own. They explain the reason for the shame we often experience. They put markers on the external standard that we instinctively feel exists and that we miss.

But there is a way of making the mark. Achieving the standard that many of us have a hunch exists. The key is in the first of the Bible's Ten Commandments. The one before 'Don't do idols' says this:

You shall have no other gods before me.[17]

When Jesus explained it to the people, he put it like this: 'Love the Lord your God with all your heart and with all your soul and with all your mind.'[18] In other words, God himself asks for exclusive loyalty and devotion from us. So much so that we won't have room for anything or anyone else in the top spot. Which brings us full circle to our definition of an idol: anything that takes God's place in our lives.

Loyalty and devotion are not heavy burdens to carry when you're in a relationship. When I am loved it is easier to love. I respond to loyalty by showing it. God's offer is that kind of relationship. A relationship where we love the God who first loved us. A relationship where we make God our leader and adopt his standards. It's at that point that God gives us the power to help us do it. God doesn't leave us on our own to live life the way that he says we should. He promises to help us live it.

That is why 'Love the Lord your God' comes first in the list. Doing that plugs into the power that can help us with the rest. God himself enables us to follow his ways and to experience all the benefits that come with them. God really can make the impossible possible.

I remember clearly standing at the front of the church, in front of hundreds of people, minutes before Rachel and I were declared 'husband and wife'. The whole wedding felt like a massive deal, especially the vows. I remember repeating them, after the minister, line by meaning-charged line. It was as if there was an echo in the building, as I repeated the promise. I heard it again inside my head, as I comprehended its enormity and difficulty: 'Love ... honour ... forsake all others ... be faithful only to her ...'

I remember the minister describing them as 'impossible'. He was right. They were. As you read this, I wouldn't want you to think that I'm writing as one who finds this easy, who has life and love taped. Rather as a fellow struggler. Those vows have been 'impossible'. I have failed at times to love as I should, to give unselfishly as I promised.

Two things are clear to me. I can't help myself. My own attempts at self-improvement make no lasting difference. When I've kept God outside and uninvolved, I've often failed. But when I've considered his standards and asked for his help to meet them, things have been better. I've been different.

Accepting God's leadership means accepting his forgiveness too. The God who sets the standard is able to forgive us when we fail. That's why there's always the opportunity for a new start. Nothing is too much for him to deal with. Nothing.

And if you're there, right now, thinking, 'Yeah, but you don't know about me', then you're right, I don't. But God does. If you're looking at a long list of targets and failed promises and having to tell yourself that keeping one is 'good progress', then all I can do is offer you God's laws of life. And more importantly the forgiveness that's on offer for having broken them.

4. What would Jesus say to George Michael?

As a member of Wham! or as a solo artist, George Michael has rarely been out of the headlines. The number-one records, the massive success of his album *Faith* in America, and the legal battle with his former record company Sony have all kept him in the public eye.

Then, in April 1998, George hit the headlines for very different reasons. He was arrested in the toilets of Will Rogers Park in Beverley Hills for engaging in a lewd act. He was later convicted of the offence and fined. The incident led to him coming out as homosexual, and, as George said himself, 'Running naked up and down Oxford Street, singing "I Am What I Am" would have been a more dignified way to come out.'[1]

In reading the papers at that time I felt genuinely sorry for George Michael. He found himself in an awful situation which few of us will ever have to endure. What marks him out as different from the rest of us is very simple. He got caught. Most of us don't.

It's an uncomfortable thought. I'm not for a moment suggesting that most of us could have been caught in the same sort of situation as George. But Jesus tells us something that puts this incident into a perspective that we find shocking, and perhaps even offensive.

Jesus is seated on a mountainside and is teaching the crowds on a variety of subjects. He starts talking about adultery. 'You have heard that it was said, "Do not commit adultery."'[2] (When Jesus talks about adultery he isn't just talking about being unfaithful to your husband or wife. He's talking about sex with anyone who isn't your husband or wife.)

These words are a challenge to George Michael, but they're also a challenge to the rest of us. Because here comes the truly shocking part, 'But I tell you that anyone who looks at a woman lustfully has already committed adultery with her in his heart.'[3]

It's bad enough that Jesus speaks out against sex outside marriage. That probably sounds terribly restrictive to a lot of us. But then he adds that to look lustfully at someone outside that marriage relationship is like committing adultery with him or her in your heart.

I read those words and, frankly, they trouble me. If this is the standard that Jesus is talking about, I know that I'm a miserable failure. I'm sure I'm not unique in feeling uncomfortable at Jesus' words here. In fact I seriously doubt whether anyone can stand up and declare himself or herself innocent on this score.

But do you see that Jesus tells us here that whether we are arrested for lewd behaviour in a park, or caught looking lustfully at members of the opposite sex, we're in the same boat? And it's the *Titanic*! Jesus tells us that we don't measure up to God's standards – that morally we're all failures. Some of us might fail more dramatically, or more publicly, than others. But we're all guilty. Which makes throwing the first stone of judgment as some sort of innocent bystander difficult, to say the least! So to start with, I think Jesus would want to point out that we're all of us guilty of failing to live up to God's standards and in no position to condemn a person from a position of high moral superiority.

Secondly, I think Jesus would want to point out an incident from his dealings with a woman caught making a mess of God's rules for sex.

You'd think that Jesus, as God in the flesh, would get on well with the most religious people that he came into contact with. In fact he had some spectacular run-ins with them. The Pharisees were perhaps the most respected religious people of the time. They were pious men who gave away a tenth of their income. They even went to the extreme of giving away a tenth of the herbs that they had. Imagine their attention to detail! 'Here is a tenth of the mint that's growing in my garden.'

But they were rather too pleased with themselves. They loved to be greeted and honoured in public. They enjoyed performing their acts of charity in full view of others, for their good deeds to be applauded.

They adored being seen in the best seats, the seats of honour. Outwardly they were amazingly religious people. Inwardly they stank; their motives had become very suspect. Jesus pointed this out to them forcefully. He likened them to whitewashed tombs, clean on the outside, stinking and rotten inside.[4]

This wasn't the best way to win the friendship of most Pharisees!

One day the Pharisees and the teachers of the law set a trap for Jesus. They brought Jesus a woman caught in adultery and challenged him over whether she should be stoned or not. (Notice that the man she was caught in adultery with is nowhere to be seen!) This is one of the better-known stories in the Bible. Jesus' reaction to the question is curious to say the least. Here's how John records the event in his biography of Jesus:

> Jesus bent down and wrote with his finger in the dirt. They kept at him, badgering him. He straightened up and said, 'The sinless one among you, go first: Throw the stone.' Bending down again he wrote some more in the dirt.
>
> Hearing that, they walked away, one after another, beginning with the oldest. The woman was left alone. Jesus stood up and spoke to her. 'Woman, where are they? Does no one condemn you?'
>
> 'No one, Master.'
>
> 'Neither do I,' said Jesus. 'Go on your way. From now on, don't sin.'[5]

Wouldn't we love to know what it was that Jesus was writing in the dust on the ground with his finger? Was he writing the Ten Commandments as a reminder of the ways that his questioners were less than perfect themselves? Was he writing about specific incidents in the lives of those who surrounded him? We have no idea what it is that he wrote. But his reply to the question he is asked is devastating.

'If any of you are free from sin, go ahead, stone her.' (That word 'sin' is the one that the Bible uses for falling short of God's standards, or for being in rebellion to God – cutting him out of the way that we live.) Faced with that challenge, it's the older ones, the wiser ones, who drift off first. Soon the only people there are the woman and Jesus.

This idea of sin is an important one to understand. Lots of us like to think that sin is what we read about in the tabloids. Or perhaps the yardstick that we use is that so long as we've never hurt anyone we're OK. When Jesus uses the term he means something completely different.

George Michael's album *Older* contains a song, 'To Be Forgiven', that talks about the need that the singer has to be saved from himself; how his life is like a river, sweeping him along out of control. He wants to cry out for help, but is frightened to. The song concludes that he's drowning, and as he sinks he would beg to be forgiven, if he knew what his sin was.

The message that Jesus would want George Michael to understand is that he, like each one of us, needs to know his sin. Whatever his individual acts of sin might be, the root of all of the wrong things that he does are his basic attitude: shutting God out of his life. By living life in rebellion to his maker, George is, in that most old-fashioned of preachers' terms, a sinner or a rebel. In common with the rest of the human race.

I don't think that Jesus would want to leave it there, though. Jesus would want George to see the rest of the story too, because it gives us a fantastic insight into his attitude towards people like us.

What does Jesus do about the woman he is confronted with in the story? This is a moment of high tension. The Christian belief in Jesus as God in human form means that the woman is in fact face to face with the one person ever who was without sin. The one person who could throw the stones. And yet he doesn't. Instead he tells her that he doesn't condemn her either.

The story of the woman caught in adultery is truly a parable for our times. We love tolerance. We intensely dislike it when people judge us. George has described his relief at 'being seen in my worst possible incarnation and people being alright with it.'[6]

Jesus shows the most tremendous compassion and love for this woman, who is caught in the most shameful circumstances. As with George Michael, she got caught. But if you or I had our most private thoughts projected on to a cinema screen, we'd go through the shame of it all too. Jesus would certainly want to point out to George the love and compassion that he has for him.

We make a mistake, though, if we think that Jesus displays tolerance when he doesn't condemn the woman caught in the act of adultery. He shows amazing compassion and shows her great pity. But not tolerance. He still emphasizes that there is a moral code, and that she has broken it.

Here's the bit that we don't like. 'Go now and leave your life of sin.' Jesus doesn't condemn her. But he does warn her to leave her old life of rebellion towards God and start living in the way God designed for her. His words are compassionate, but at the same time a passionate warning. I think that these are words that Jesus would use in talking to George Michael. 'I don't condemn you – but start living differently.'

Some might expect Jesus to reproach George Michael over his homosexuality, and there's obviously an issue there. But I think that Jesus would be more concerned with cutting to the core issue. Contrary to the opinions of some, we are not ultimately defined as people by our sexuality, but by our relationship with God.

I think Jesus might point to a well-known story from the Old Testament. George Michael is without a doubt an exceptional songwriter. But this story concerns a poet and musician who was even better known, even more gifted.

David was the King of Israel, an immensely important figure in the Old Testament. With candid honesty, the Bible records incidents in David's life which are more shocking than those from George

Michael's.[7] David has wives and concubines galore. He has great wealth. He wants for nothing. But while he's out walking on the roof of his palace one evening he sees a woman bathing. Bathsheba is very beautiful. Even though he knows she's married to one of the soldiers who are away fighting a war for him, David sends for her and sleeps with her.

The king of Israel has committed adultery. Then, to make things worse, David gets news that must have left him with his heart in his mouth. Bathsheba sends him a message: 'I am pregnant.'

Now David is in serious trouble. As the chief judge in the land, he knows that the penalty for adultery is death. So David tries to cover his tracks. He sends for Bathsheba's husband Uriah, on the pretext of wanting a report on how the war is going. David sits there and pretends to listen to what Uriah reports, but is in reality just waiting to be done with the problem of Uriah finding out that Bathsheba is pregnant. David has a plan in place to cover his tracks.

There's a theory held by some sports coaches that athletes in a competition should refrain from sex for the duration of a tournament. The belief is that they will then give their best in the sporting arena. In the same way, it was David's practice to enforce the same rule of no sex for his soldiers while they were at war.[8]

However, David orders Uriah to go home to Bathsheba. The plan is very simple. After his time away at war, Uriah and his wife are reunited. They'll sleep together, and the baby that Bathsheba is expecting will be assumed to be Uriah's.

There's only one problem. Uriah turns out to be an extraordinary man of principle. He still considers himself to be on duty, and he doesn't go home. Instead he sleeps at the entrance to the palace. David hears of this and tries again the next night, getting Uriah drunk first. Still Uriah doesn't go home.

David then gets desperate. He sends Uriah back to the battlefront, and as he does so he carries with him his own death warrant. David sends with Uriah the instructions for the commander of the battle forces to place Uriah where the fighting is at his most fierce. And then for the rest of David's troops to withdraw. There's no doubt about it. David knowingly sent Uriah to his death.

Let's be honest, if we were to read David's story in the newspaper rather than the Bible, we'd be even more scandalized than we already are. If this was the Prime Minister of Great Britain or the President of the United States, you can imagine the news coverage! Although we can't be sure these days, this would probably cost them their jobs.

Well, thanks to some skilled public relations, including a special hour-long *Parkinson* show, it seems that most people are still buying George's CDs. There was plenty of speculation at the time of his arrest that this incident could cost George a lot in terms of lost sales. Would music buyers forgive him? If you find it difficult to imagine forgiveness for George Michael, you'll find it even harder to imagine that David could be forgiven.

Nathan, a very brave man, went to David and pointed out God's displeasure at David's actions.

David's reply was simple. David realized that he'd been playing to his own rules rather than God's. 'I have sinned against the LORD.'[9]

He was deadly serious in his regret and spent seven days fasting and praying. This time of trauma produced some of the most heartfelt poetry the world has ever seen. Psalm 51 is titled, 'A psalm of David. When the prophet Nathan came to him after David had committed adultery with Bathsheba.' The opening lines of the psalm show a profound and very real sorrow for the way he's made such a mess of things.

> Have mercy on me, O God,
>   according to your unfailing love;
> according to your great compassion
>   blot out my transgressions.
> Wash away all my iniquity
>   and cleanse me from my sin.
>
> For I know my transgressions,
>   and my sin is always before me.
> Against you, you only, have I sinned
>   and done what is evil in your sight ... [10]

A few days after his arrest, George Michael was interviewed on the CNN television station. On the show he talked about the incident being 'humiliating and embarrassing'. Most of us are glad that we don't know how humiliating it must be to be caught in the sort of situation he was in.

It would be inaccurate to paint George as a man

who was weighed down by regrets about the way he behaved, though. Because as well as finding his arrest humiliating and embarrassing, he also described it as 'funny to some degree'. He also commented that 'I'm a very proud man – I want people to know that I feel stupid and I feel reckless and weak for having allowed my sexuality to be exposed this way, but I don't feel any shame whatsoever.'[11]

The psalm we've just looked at shows us that David knew all about regrets. And I think that Jesus would want George, and every one of us, to sit down and learn from this story.

Because ultimately it is a story that shows that if we turn from what we've done wrong and ask God for his forgiveness, he'll give it to us. David knew all about that too, and expressed it in his songs. Another of those, Psalm 32, sums it up well:

> Blessed is he
>   whose transgressions are forgiven,
>   whose sins are covered.
> Blessed is the man
>   whose sin the LORD does not count
>   against him …
>
> Then I acknowledged my sin to you
>   and did not cover up my iniquity.
> I said, 'I will confess
>   my transgressions to the LORD' –
> and you forgave
>   the guilt of my sin.[12]

Finally, I think that Jesus would want to tell George Michael this. That regardless of whether some of those who buy his CDs forgive George or not, God offers forgiveness. It's shown graphically in the story of David and Bathsheba. It's as true to today as it was then. That's the message that Jesus would want to give George Michael. God is still in the business of forgiveness.

5. What would Jesus say to Geri Halliwell?

Others of the Spice Girls have had more embarrassing moments on the way to the top. Posh Spice had a role as a roller-skating sperm in a BBC science series and Baby Spice was once the girlfriend of the Milky Bar Kid. But these are less well known than Ginger Spice's past as a Turkish gameshow host and 'glamour' model.

Geri Halliwell was always the Spice Girl who grabbed the most headlines. Whether it was meeting Mandela or kissing Prince Charles, speaking out on family planning or falling out of her dress at the Brit Awards, the artist formerly known as Ginger Spice was usually right in the thick of it.

It's a long way from Watford, where she felt she was the token poor girl at her school, to the height of Spice Mania. And easy to forget the impact the group had. They were the only artists to have their first six singles reach number one in Britain. 'Wannabe' was the first debut single by a British act to make it to number one in America. They had number-one singles in twenty-three countries. Tours sold out, and merchandizing became so successful that it became a challenge to buy things that *weren't* endorsed by the Spice Girls. Even *Spiceworld the Movie* (surely conceived as a tax loss?) went to number two in the US, stopped from hitting the top spot only by *Titanic*. Then, on video, 220,000 copies were sold in Britain alone – in the first week of its release!

It must have been a difficult decision to walk away from all of that. It was headline news when Geri did. She likened her experience to 'standing on this mountain top, and I jumped, not knowing where I was going to fall ... I had to go, to get my feet back on the ground.'[1]

You have to feel for Geri in the confusion she was in after she left the Spice Girls. Leaving any job is stressful enough. Quite what it must be like to walk away from something so high-profile, where everyone has an opinion, is impossible to say. Having taken the decision to leave a group as fuelled by hype as hers, it was inevitable that there would be massive interest in her departure, the reason for it, and the future for Geri and the rest of the group.

On top of all that, of course, this wasn't just a job. Walking out meant leaving behind the group and cutting the friendships with other members. Not going to Victoria and David's wedding, hearing Mel B say, 'We don't need her anymore.' The sense of loneliness and disorientation that followed leaving the band must have been incredibly hard to handle.

For the year since leaving the Spice Girls she talked about having 'been in mourning, re-evaluating myself',[2] yet – bravely or foolishly – she decided to go through the roller-coaster of emotions in front of an audience. Personally, the last thing I'd have wanted in those circumstances would have been a film-maker in tow as well. Geri thought otherwise. What started as a personal video diary became a film. At first Molly Dineen was puzzled by the request to produce it, unsure about its purpose: 'From the start, I didn't know what it was about. Geri would say, "It's about *me*!" and I'd say, "Yes. And?" ... The problem for Geri was that in the end it was Ginger that was famous, not her. The frustration is you want people to know what *you're* like.'[3]

Doing the film may or may not have been a wise move. Clearly Geri wanted to stay in the public eye, and it seems that the old desire to make it to the top, or to remain there, was still as strong as it ever was.

But just as strong was the desire for understanding. Trying to find an answer to the question, 'What is my own identity in amongst all of this? Who is Geri Halliwell?' One thing's for sure, she put to death the cartoon character that was Ginger Spice. Ginger was based on her wild-child days. Geri had outgrown the role, and flogging off the dresses she wore back then closed that particular chapter.

As she admits to Dineen's camera, 'I want some philosophical guru, a mentor', someone wise to sit down with for a one to one. So I think that Geri would appreciate talking to Jesus.

Perhaps the first thing that Jesus would do would

be to reassure Geri that he isn't in the business of adding to the pressures that she is under. One of the better-known invitations that he issued to the crowds that came to listen to him reinforces this: 'Come to me, all you who are weary and burdened, and I will give you rest. Take my yoke upon you and learn from me, for I am gentle and humble in heart, and you will find rest for your souls. For my yoke is easy and my burden is light.'[4]

At the time Jesus was speaking, oxen were yoked in a wooden frame to get them to plough together, in the way that a team of horses might be reined together to pull a carriage. Jesus promises those who are tempted to look to him that he isn't in the business of adding to any burden they are already under. His yoke isn't heavy. Following him is, in fact, a lot less effort than running yourself ragged in pursuit of finding your self-esteem or self-worth anywhere else.

Perhaps that'd come as a surprise to Geri Halliwell. I suspect that most people think that being a follower of Jesus is about keeping a whole host of repressive rules and regulations. But Jesus himself contradicts that image, saying that any burden involved is light, and that taking on that easy yoke will result in finding rest. It's an amazing offer and quite a contrast with the yoke of fame that she struggles under.

And to be fair, Geri isn't unaware of the dangers of her high-profile life. Just after leaving the Spice Girls she spoke about the way her life had become. 'The whole fame thing, and money, is such a test of character ... This lifestyle brings out the best and worst in everybody, it sort of accelerates the extremes of personalities. It's so easy to get lost, to not keep your feet on the ground.'[5]

In the film we see some of the costs of her fame too. We see Geri hidden away, watching the paparazzi from the roof of her Parisian hotel. We watch Geri checking the newspapers to see what people's opinions of her are, and, as her assistant asks, 'Can you imagine checking the papers every morning to see if people accept you?'[6]

However well adjusted we like to think we are, we're all affected by the things people say about us, good or bad. Which is exactly why we can't base our self-esteem on the opinions of our friends and family, let alone newspaper columnists. It's an insane existence.

Geri thinks a lot about self-esteem and self-worth; they are important issues for her. She plans to write about these things in her autobiography, to be published long before she reaches the age of thirty. In Dineen's film we see that self-esteem and self-worth are the first two topics that she lists when explaining her book to her accountant. Indeed, the act of writing her autobiography can be seen as another sign of her trying to work out who she is, make some sense of the past, and look to the future.

That desire for self-esteem and self-worth is highlighted in some of the things that she records on her 'cosmic shopping lists'. Having read Louise Hay's *I Can Heal Your Life*, Geri has made it a practice to write down the things that she wants from life. Here are a couple that we learn from Molly Dineen's film: 'I feel love, security and oneness with everything – especially myself.' 'I am admired and respected by the whole world.'

At one time it seemed that the girl who was only ever a donkey or a shepherd in her school nativity play had found that love and admiration in the screaming affirmation of fans. This was probably something that she missed post-Spice Girls. After she sold the dresses she'd worn as Ginger Spice at the Sotheby's sale, she got another taste of it, pushing her way through a scrum of photographers and fans to declare, 'I feel ecstatic and charged. I felt loved.'

But the problem with fame is the downside – that if you flourish on public approval you'll wilt when it turns to disapproval. One thing that seemed certain from the film, and was confirmed by her PA, was that during the year after the Spice split, Geri was still famous, but she wasn't very happy. Although it might seem absurd even to suggest it, having earned an estimated £13 million from her career with the Spices, you couldn't help thinking that it wasn't a trade worth making.

I strongly suspect that Jesus would cut to the heart of the problem. And not by addressing the immediate issue of self-image or personal identity, either. Those close to Jesus knew what it meant to have a sense of peace. Jesus might well point out to Geri Halliwell, 'You're looking for contentment; it's missing from your life. Why don't you look at what some of those who know me have found, that by following me they find a peace of mind that they never knew before?' Perhaps Jesus would point Geri in the direction of something that one of his earliest followers once wrote: 'I have learned to be content whatever the circumstances. I know what it is to be in need, and I know what it is to have plenty. I have learned the secret of being content in any and every situation, whether well fed or hungry, whether living in plenty or in want.'[7]

These are remarkable words written by someone who went through a remarkable transformation. As Saul, he was the most zealous of Jews, in both his religious education and the strict practice of his faith. In fact he took it to the very limit and made it his goal to rid Judaism of these heretical Christians, seeking out believers in order to have them put to death. It's saying something, but Saul could have taught Geri a thing or two about dedication and ambition.

Yet something happened to him and he changed his name to Paul. His life turned right around. As Paul, he spread the message about Jesus that he'd previously been trying to quash. And the people he'd once sided with were now out to get him. Now he writes from a prison cell, having been arrested yet again for teaching people about his Christian faith. So when Paul writes about being content whatever his circumstances, in plenty or in poverty, these really are powerful words.

So what's his secret? It's got to be one that's worth being let in on, hasn't it? Geri wants to know how to be content. To escape measuring how she defines her own self-worth through the opinion of other people.

No longer to have to check the newspapers or look to family or be seen to be doing good for some indication that you are loved. But she's hardly unique in that, is she? We all want to be loved, we want to be admired. We try to boost our sense of self-worth, because so many of us are fundamentally dissatisfied with who we are. In our western culture, we've turned life into a competition for self-esteem.

And that's the root cause of our misery, because such a system will always point out that each of us is a loser every time someone else is on the front page, or each time an unfavourable word is spoken about us. In his study, *New Britain on the Couch*, Dr Oliver James highlights that Britain is less happy than it was in 1950, despite being considerably better off in material terms.[8] One of his conclusions was that it's the culture of competition that we live in that has created this dissatisfaction. If we're defined by what we achieve then very few of us will die happy. Because there's always another accolade just around the corner, another achievement a little further on. It has to lead to discontent if we're always comparing ourselves unfavourably with those above us – rather than counting our blessings.

Molly Dineen's purpose in the film *Geri* was to show that this way of living is futile. 'What I wanted to show was that what she's chasing ultimately is elusive. There's the dream, but it's empty.'[9] Yet Paul, in prison and quite probably cold, damp, and hungry, talks about being satisfied whatever his circumstances. The prisoner seems to have found freedom. He describes himself as content, which is bewildering to most of us.

The next line of his letter gives the game away. 'I can do everything through him who gives me strength.'[10] He doesn't mean that he's like some superhero with unlimited powers. But he says, 'I can cope with all things. Because of Jesus.' Paul has found a personal security that doesn't need to be bolstered.

Jesus would want to impress upon Geri Halliwell that she could know the same solid foundation to her life too. That whatever she feels about herself, he loves her deeply. Sadly, I think that Geri would have trouble accepting it. At the root of all her problems, as for so many who seek self-esteem and self-worth, she has the fear that she isn't worth very much. In common with so many, Geri struggles with not feeling good enough.

Cynics suspected her motives for accepting the invitation to work with the United Nations. Wasn't it simply to remain in the public eye? The truth was more complicated than that. Partly she was fuelled by a desire to do something good with her fame, to make a difference in the world.

But Geri also described going to the UN as one of the happiest days of her life, because of all of her achievements, this was the one that impressed her mother the most. 'For the first time in my life my mother is proud of me.'[11] (So much for girl power!) We see Geri, sitting delighted at her initial briefing with UN officials, asking, 'What made you pick me?' She can hardly get her head around the fact that the wannabe from Watford has been chosen for such a prestigious and high-profile role. How much it means to her is revealed in her comment, 'This is going to give my life meaning … it takes the emphasis off whether I'm good enough.'[12]

If she's astonished that the UN chose her, it's going to be a lot more difficult for her to believe that she is loved by the God of the whole universe. But Jesus would want to underline to Geri that his love for her isn't just wishful thinking; it's for real.

Paul had an inner power that few of us have, based on something so much stronger than the whim of people's opinion of him – even if those people are powerful and working for the UN. His inner strength meant that whatever his circumstances he was content. Because he knew Jesus and because knowing Jesus was enough. He didn't need to create a sense of self-worth from anything else. His sense of being valuable wasn't based on what he had – just as well, because he didn't have very much! His sense of significance wasn't based on accolades – again a good thing given the number of people who wanted him dead. God had come to earth in human form and demonstrated the love he had for him by going as far as dying a horrible death on a cross for him. That was enough for him; he didn't need anything else to tell him he was worth something. He was worth everything, he was loved. God said so, and had demonstrated it in the most powerful way. What more could he want?

What more can you want? If you can't be content with that, what will make you content? Even if fame *was* satisfying and *could* make you complete, it looks pretty empty held up against this, doesn't it?

Knowing that the God of the universe says you are worth sending Jesus for makes a few number ones and getting to appear on *Top of the Pops* suddenly seem like very small beer, doesn't it?

At the times she has been most down in her life, Geri has had the sense that she's missing something. 'I think everyone's got a void [in their life] to a degree if we really sat down, an unconnection with God or with the world ... Maybe it's simpler than that, maybe I just want some love in my life.'[13]

Jesus would tell Geri Halliwell that he is the connection with God that she's lacking, and that to respond to him would lead to the only pure love she's ever experienced in her life. The God of the universe loves her; she'll never be rejected as not good enough. Who cares what the tabloids think?

6. What would Jesus say to Richard Branson?

When *Friends* came to London for Ross's wedding, he was one of the choices for a guest part, along with Fergie. According to research 98% of us know who Richard Branson is. He's recognized all over the world, usually by his trademark smile and woolly jumper. Ninety-nine per cent of us recognize the Virgin brand name. It's ubiquitous and unites a bewildering array of products.

You can wake in the morning to Virgin Radio and apply your Virgin Vie cosmetics. You can then take a Virgin train to a Virgin hotel for your first meeting of the day. Arrive at the airport for your Virgin Atlantic flight. Arrive on the other side of the pond, after listening to a V2 CD, and browse in a Virgin Megastore. After business is complete, you look for your wedding dress at Virgin Bride and the dream honeymoon with Virgin Holidays, all of which can be financed through Virgin Direct. You unwind at the end of a 'virgin day' with a Virgin cola. The pundits predict that Virgin will become one of the leading global brands of the twenty-first century.

And to think that it all started with a student magazine in the 1960s. From there Richard Branson went on to run a mail-order record business, then a record label. The first artist to be signed was Mike Oldfield, whose album *Tubular Bells* is reputed to have kept the label afloat in the early years. Now Virgin has spread across the globe and Richard Branson heads up a multi-billion-pound business with all the trappings of success, including a private holiday home on his very own tropical island.

No-one really knows what he is worth in financial terms; analysts are left to guess. As it was reported in 1997, 'His personal wealth reportedly totals $2.7 billion, but it's hard to get an accurate tally, since his companies are private and are constantly dividing and multiplying, with Branson launching new ventures on what sometimes seems like a daily basis.'[1]

It's safe to say, though, that Richard Branson is a man of exceptional wealth and power. Usually such men are subject to ridicule, envy, jealousy. Yet Richard Branson is fantastically popular. The pollsters asked, 'Who do people think should run the country?' Top answer in the survey – Richard Branson. Who should be the first mayor of London? Most popular choice – Richard Branson. Who do young people most aspire to be like? Richard Branson. Who would be the best person to rewrite the Ten Commandments? Well, let's not get carried away here; Mother Teresa won that one. But Richard

Branson was right there at number four behind the Pope and the Archbishop of Canterbury.

Richard Branson is a man who apparently has everything – fame, fortune, family and friends. That's important because so often the people who know great success pay for it in another area of their lives. Relationships, recreation and health can all wind up footing the bill. The chances are that you know someone who has shelled out that kind of expense for his or her success.

But it appears that Richard Branson is different. He dotes on a family who in his words would 'kill for each other', and enjoys plenty of highly publicized recreation. Despite some of his more adventurous escapades and a demanding business schedule, he remains healthy. And as if that isn't enough, Richard Branson clearly enjoys himself. The future's bright. Success really does seem to have brought him everything.

So what would Jesus say to Richard Branson? Branson is a success by any standard of reckoning, isn't he? He's vastly rich, and relatively young. He seems to have the world at his feet – he seems to have everything he could possibly want. What could Jesus possibly have to offer him?

Well, I think Jesus would start by talking about money. He talked about money more than nearly any other subject, and, contrary to popular opinion, he never said it was a bad thing to have. At the same time Jesus helped people get the right perspective on its importance and warned people of the dangers of inflating its value. Perhaps Jesus would start here:

'Richard, I want to remind you not to bank on success. It's crucial that you measure success accurately. And the usual way might not be the best.' Dollars or sterling (or even the euro!) may be the most conventional means of measurement, but they can give a false reading. Don't be blinded by your bank statements, because if you are, the really important things get lost.'

Jesus told a story about a man who seemed to have life taped. Business was so good that he had to tear down his storehouse to build bigger ones in order to store all his grain and goods. And he said to himself, 'You have plenty of good things laid up for many years. Take life easy; eat, drink and be merry.'

But God said to him, 'You fool! This very night your life will be demanded from you. Then who will get what you have prepared for yourself?'[2]

If we are driven by the need to succeed financially, we can lose sight of the fact that life is about more than the accumulation of stuff. The winner isn't the person who dies with the most toys. There's another dimension. Here Jesus reminds us that whatever we strive to earn, we can't take it with us.

Mind you, people have tried! There's a story of a man who insisted that he be buried in his pink Cadillac. The day of his funeral came and a crowd gathered to witness the man seated in his car, dressed in his best suit and hat. Someone put a cigar in his mouth and even tried to light it! As the crane lowered this successful man and his car into the ground an onlooker was heard to say, 'Wow, that's really living!'

Success isn't worth a great deal if you can't take it

with you, and I think Jesus would want to remind Richard Branson of this. And I think that Branson would probably agree. Like most of us, he's sat down and wondered about it all. And around the time of his fortieth birthday he had cause to reflect on where his life was heading.

> I was ... at an all time low. I'd seemed to have run out of a purpose in my life. I'd proved myself to myself in many areas. I'd just turned forty. I was seeking a new challenge. I was even considering selling up everything except for the airline. Being able to focus on one business venture that I loved. But also to have the time to try to use my business skills to tackle issues that I felt I could help, such as in attacking the cigarette companies, cervical cancer, etc.
> I felt I'd get better self-satisfaction in this way and would not be wasting the next forty years of my life just running companies ... a repeat of the first forty years.[3]

Like most of us he's sat down and wondered about it all. Despite his wealth, status, and age he was experiencing a sense of it all being meaningless. What was the point?

There's a man that Jesus talks to who was in a very similar situation. Someone who was young, had great riches, and yet seemed to sense that he didn't have it all. As he surveyed his life, he sensed that ultimately it wasn't enough. And so his thoughts turned to eternal life and how he might gain that. He gets the chance to meet Jesus, and when he does he asks him a question: 'Teacher, what good thing must I do to get eternal life?'[4]

It's a great question, isn't it? The biggest question in the world. It's a question that if we're honest, most of us have thought about from time to time. We may have phrased it differently: 'How do I get to heaven?' or 'There has to be more than this.' But very few of us have never wondered about the answer. Sadly, most people who do ask think about it for a little while and then tell themselves not to be so silly. They turn the telly back on or go out with friends, faintly embarrassed at having entertained such thoughts. Others try hard to ponder how to grasp eternal life, and give up — it's all too difficult and complicated, and who's to know? For others the demands of the immediate can fill the diary, occupy the mind and squeeze out thoughts of the eternal.

This question that the rich young man asks, 'Teacher, what good thing must I do to get eternal life?' is fascinating. I hope I'm not being too harsh on him, but perhaps he was ready to make a big gesture. He had lots of money — what did he have to do to get eternal life? Frank Sinatra was reputed to be ready to do this in his old age. He was ready to give half of his wealth to the Catholic Church in return for an audience with the Pope. Or perhaps the rich man was ready, like Richard Branson, to put his financial clout behind some project for the good of the disadvantaged.

Jesus' reply, as is so often the case, shows that the question is based on entirely the wrong supposition.

The question asks, 'What good thing can I do?' What good works will get me into heaven, how do I earn my ticket? The question assumes that it is within reach of the individual, that if we try really hard and are good enough we'll become acceptable to God – we'll be good enough for heaven. The way that Jesus answers him makes it clear; that's not the way it works. 'If you want to enter life, obey the commandments.' That's all there is to it!

The rich man must have been disappointed; he was probably waiting for a new spiritual insight, or at least something to do – something that would get him eternal life. The last thing he would have expected would have been to be directed back to the Ten Commandments. But that's what Jesus does.

You see, Jesus knows what this man's problem is. He's too self-confident. He's used to succeeding; he's used to achieving what he sets out to do. So Jesus sets him an impossible task.

The rich man's reply is interesting: 'All these I have kept. What do I still lack?'

It's telling that he realizes that he still lacks something and that he asks Jesus what that something is. The answer is that the rich man lacks something in the way of self-awareness!

God's standards are the very highest. This is why, when Jesus says if you want to do it by your own efforts, you 'only' need to keep the Ten Commandments. What he's trying to get straight for the rich man is that his place in heaven cannot be earned. It's no good hoping that our grand gestures will somehow impress God. For a start, our good deeds aren't really that good. The Bible warns us that our good deeds are like filthy rags before God. A better translation for 'filthy rags' would be 'dirty nappies'.[5] However great our gestures might be in our own eyes, they aren't good enough for God.

But the rich man doesn't get it. He thinks he's kept all the commandments. He's never murdered, never committed adultery, he's always honoured his mother and father ... He hasn't understood it at all.

Just to take the first two examples, Jesus has already told his listeners that if you are angry with someone you have failed and are subject to judgment. That if you just look lustfully at a person you're guilty of committing adultery with him or her in your heart.[6] It sounds almost ludicrous to us, but that's the whole point! When you look at the standards for living that Jesus sets, you realize that you haven't kept the commandments; you've broken them time after time – we've all broken them on a daily basis.

So Jesus points out to the rich young man again, in a different way, that he isn't perfect. 'If you want to be perfect, go, sell all your possessions and give to the poor, and you will have treasure in heaven. Then come, follow me.'

The man heard this and he went away sad, because he was a very wealthy man.[7]

Jesus would want to say to Richard Branson, as he says here to the rich man, that you can't earn it. Being rich isn't any help towards attaining eternal life. In fact it's a hindrance. That was a revolutionary thought to the disciples and the rest of Jesus' listeners. They thought the rich were especially blessed by God, that their wealth was a sign of God's approval of them.

Then Jesus drops a bombshell: 'It's easier to get a camel through the eye of a needle than for a rich man to enter the kingdom of God.'[8]

I think that this points to Jesus having a sense of humour, but more importantly you couldn't hear a story like this and forget it. Or forget the point he's making. Jesus is saying that it's incredibly hard for a rich man or woman to enter the kingdom – where God and his goodness reign supreme.

Most of us have played that game, haven't we, where we make plans about how we would spend a £1 million Lottery win? We decide on the car, the house, how much we'd save, how much we'd give away, who we'd give it to. And the reason that the Lottery is so attractive to millions of people is that it represents the chance of a great deal of cash and, with it, some security.

These are powerful motivators. People queued around the block to buy tickets in July 1998 when an American lottery jackpot had accumulated to a world record £180 million. In fact the syndicate that won made the effort of taking a round trip of 100 miles over the state border to buy their tickets. We know that the odds of it being us are tiny; in the case in America someone worked out that you had more chance of being struck by lightening – fourteen times! – than of winning that jackpot. But thoughts of the money and the security that it provides bring us out in droves.

You see, the greatest danger that money and great wealth bring is that we equate money with security. Money can so easily make you independent. Of other people, and more seriously, of God. If you think you can fix most problems by throwing money at them, you don't think you need God. You think you're comfortable, that you're secure. High achievers beware. Are you the 'no problem too big, no hill too steep' type? Are you the troubleshooter, the person others look to for solutions? If so, you're likely to be especially prone to thinking that you are in control, the master or mistress of your destiny.

The danger of that thinking – that you don't need God in your life – is a far greater danger than anything that Richard Branson has ever faced in his attempts to fly his balloon around the world. Jesus would want to warn Richard Branson about this. By any objective standard, Richard Branson is rich. He has more money than I can even imagine. In thinking about what Jesus would say to Richard Branson, he'd warn him that he can't serve God and money. That's why the disciples, greatly astonished, say, 'Who then can be saved?'[9] If the rich can't do it, what chance do we have?

Jesus looked at them (the word used suggests that he looked at his disciples long and hard – it was important that they remembered this), and said: 'With man this is impossible, but with God all things are possible.'[10]

You see, the primary point of this story isn't about money. Jesus' conversation with the rich man tells us something even more fundamental. That there's no way you'll get into the kingdom of heaven under your own steam. However great your wealth or your merits, you won't be allowed in because of some great moral act you've performed.

It's only when you ask God to forgive you for making a mess of life on your own and start living as a follower of Jesus that you'll have eternal life, which Jesus defined as knowing the only true God, and Jesus Christ, whom God sent.[11]

Jesus also calls this 'life to the full',[12] something which Richard Branson repeatedly states in his autobiography he wants. 'Life to the full' happens when God gets involved. You see, Christianity is not about forgoing wealth in this world in the hope of some heavenly consolation in the next. It's about having the fullest life on earth now. About the peace and joy of living the way we were created to – in relation to God. That might not show itself on your bank balance, but is something far richer. Living a life with God is a far fuller experience than anything Branson will ever experience, even on his tropical island.

And it's a fantastic deal! Jesus has described the joy of finding peace with God in terms that leave us in no doubt that it puts money in the shade.

> The kingdom of heaven is like treasure hidden in a field. When a man found it, he hid it again, and then in his joy went and sold all he had and bought that field.
>
> Again, the kingdom of heaven is like a merchant looking for fine pearls. When he

found one of great value, he went away and sold everything he had and bought it.[13]

To the best of my knowledge there isn't yet a Virgin Pearlbrokers; perhaps it's just a matter of time. But as a businessman, Richard Branson would recognize the scenario. Being offered a deal so good that you sell whatever you have to clinch it. Even if it means selling everything.

Jesus would tell Richard Branson that knowing God is far from being a dour, lifeless experience. The man who found the treasure, and the pearl merchant, both recognized a bargain when they saw one. In their joy at finding something of such immense value, they acted quickly. This wasn't a sacrifice for them; they were acting in their own self-interest. This made perfect business sense; they'd discovered something far more valuable than the stuff that they were already accumulating. That's how Jesus describes the kingdom of heaven.

Of course, we read the story where Jesus tells the rich young man to sell all his stuff and think, 'Yeah, Richard Branson needs to sort himself out.' But be careful! Look at it on a worldwide scale. Aren't you and I the rich as well? The very fact that you've bought a book that millions couldn't afford marks you and me out as the rich, however tight our budgets. I've a feeling that the challenge that Jesus issues to Richard Branson is one that we all face.

7. What would Jesus say to Steven Spielberg?

The door opens. The keenly anticipated encounter is about to begin. Steven Spielberg has arrived for his next meeting. In the conference rooms of Dream-Works SKG (the studio he created), waiting for Spielberg is considered a privilege.

DreamWorks SKG is confirmation, if confirmation were needed, of his inordinate success. He is, in the view of Hollywood, one of the biggest ever. Beginning with the 1975 summer horror-adventure *Jaws*, he has directed and produced a string of top-grossing films including *ET*, *Close Encounters of the Third Kind*, the *Indiana Jones* and *Back to the Future* films, *Schindler's List*, *Saving Private Ryan*, *Jurassic Park*, *Men in Black* and *Deep Impact*. There was *The Flintstones* too, but then nobody's perfect. It's a fantastic body of work, and success has brought him respect and a great deal of clout. Financially he's done extremely well too; it's estimated that through directing alone he has hauled in a phenomenal $5 billion.[1]

Not bad for a guy who obtained a 'C' in his television production course, and quite a contrast to 'Spielberg, the early years'. He made his directing debut at the age of eleven, when he used his father's wind-up camera to shoot short films of flying saucers and Second World War battles. It wasn't long before he'd enlisted his entire family to sell tickets and make lemonade for living-room showings, although the profit margins were not what he has grown accustomed to: 'It cost me about $50 to make the movie, and I would charge a quarter a ticket, and at the end of the summer I might have $55.'[2]

It's clear Spielberg has always had the abilities he believes are essential for a good director – a soaring imagination and a love of storytelling. His old scoutmaster described their camping trips: 'Stevie would start telling his ghost stories and everyone would suddenly get quiet ...'[3] Today, Spielberg's contract with DreamWorks allows him to leave each day in time for dinner, where he and the family construct stories around the dining-room table – started and ended by Spielberg himself.

He displayed great determination in making his directing aspirations happen. At the age of seventeen he strode past the security guard at Universal Studios sporting a suit and carrying his father's briefcase, which contained nothing but a sandwich and a couple of candy bars. He took advantage of an empty office and spent the summer on the plot, hanging out with editors and camera crew. His big break came three years later when he was offered a seven-year contract, directing television series for Universal. And the rest, as they say ...

The film establishment has venerated Steven Spielberg. He's won Academy Awards, Golden Globes, Lifetime Achievement awards and more. More significantly for him, he's received the applause of those he's portrayed – including the veterans of the D-Day landings on Omaha beach, and the Schindler Jews.

What would happen if one master storyteller met another? What would happen if Steven Spielberg met Jesus Christ? I think Jesus would want to talk to Spielberg about his work. About his pictures, his master images and his master themes.

Most directors have master images. The images that appear repeatedly in a number of films, often because they're a picture of how the director sees the world. Spielberg's master image is bright light. The light out of which the aliens walk in *Close Encounters*, the brilliant light in the doorway of ET's spaceship.

For Spielberg, the light signifies an entanglement of mystery and hope, born out of his childhood experience of watching meteor showers with his father. The scary part of that experience for Spielberg was being woken up in the middle of the night by his dad, not knowing what was happening. 'My heart was beating; I didn't know what he wanted to do. But what ... was very soothing, was watching this cosmic meteor shower. And I think from that moment on, I never looked at the sky and thought it was a bad place.'[4]

If Jesus and Spielberg could sit down and talk I'm certain that they would agree that light is a powerful image. That it can clearly communicate hope and power in the realm of the mysterious. And I think Jesus would take the opportunity to help Spielberg consider how he used it in just the same way.

'I am the light of the world. Whoever follows me will never walk in darkness, but will have the light of life.'[5]

It's a strong image that would not be lost on Steven Spielberg. Jesus made this statement about himself in the temple courtyard, during an annual harvest celebration. The courtyard would have been lit by huge torches, which symbolized the pillar of fire that led the Jewish nation across inhospitable desert thousands of years before. Jesus' message was clear: 'Just as that light led your distant relatives into their homeland, I will lead to life those who follow me.'

Jesus was offering to switch on the light that identifies the route and the destination, the light that illuminates otherwise unseen dangers and prevents us from getting lost. The light that an earlier writer celebrated when he penned: 'Your word is a lamp to my feet and a light for my path.'[6]

Jesus' words are pertinent in a day where people often look for a light to guide them and to show them the way to go. The fascination with the possibility of extraterrestrial life that Spielberg explores in films such as *Close Encounters* is a part of that. Indeed, many would argue that we could do with a visitor from beyond to make sense of what is here – a light to shine in the darkness. Yet Jesus claimed to be just that, the light from outside that pierces the gloom.

If light is Spielberg's master image, then rescue is one of his master themes, especially in his more 'down to earth' films. Even *ET* contains overtones of the messianic rescuer, but it is in films like *Schindler's List* and *Saving Private Ryan* that Spielberg time and again portrays the rescued and the rescuer.

The name 'Jesus', roughly translated, means 'God to the rescue', and I think that more than anything Jesus would want to talk to Steven Spielberg about this.

Jesus' talk of light was in the context of his talk of darkness. Of a dark world and of people with a dark side. Of course, our reflex is to freeze out such thinking. But some of Spielberg's work brings it up close and personal. Yesterday, I watched *Schindler's List* again. As before, I was repulsed. The ripping apart of families, the torture, the murder of innocents, the injustice, all are horrifying. It's not difficult to understand why Spielberg took three years off to recover.

I have in front of me a photograph taken inside Auschwitz, from a visit I made several years ago. It shows a room filled by a mountain of hairbrushes, each one representing another Auschwitz victim. The base of the pile covers the entire floor; the summit is close to the ceiling. It is hard to believe.

Towards the end of the film, after the liberation of the concentration camps, we see the commandant (played by Ralph Feinnes) hanged for his crimes against humanity. Part of me felt pleased his life was taken, that he suffered a fraction of what his victims suffered. But part of me was disturbed. Disturbed that I was pleased to see someone else die. It reminded me of another wartime story that illustrates well the reason for Jesus' rescue mission.

Dachau was a concentration camp liberated by the American army. They too found a situation of unspeakable horror. As in other liberated camps, the German soldiers and SS guards were immediately questioned. A young man who was a counsellor described the scene: 'Twelve SS soldiers were being taken through a small woodland to a hut for questioning. One American soldier offered to take them – his name was Chuck. Almost as soon as they'd disappeared into the trees, there was the rattle of gunfire and he came running back, claiming, 'They tried to escape, I shot them.''

The counsellor later described how he felt as he saw what went on: 'You know what terrified me? It was that if they asked me to escort the next group of SS guards I would have done the same as him. In fact as I looked at those guards and all that they had done, the horror they had perpetrated, it struck me. That the beast that was within them was within me.'

Jesus would say to Steven Spielberg, 'That's why I showed up. I've come to rescue people like that. People like you.'

The story of Oskar Schindler illustrates how we make choices for good or bad. Schindler himself made choices that helped people. Those commanding the soldiers made choices that destroyed them.

But mostly it's not as clear-cut; we don't make one type of choice all of the time. Perhaps you remember the scenes of the commandant, who for a few brief moments chooses to pardon people for what he saw as their shortcomings, before returning to his usual murderous form.

It's clear that we have freedom to choose. Freedom given to us by a God who created a world of relationships, where people lived together in community with each other and with God himself. It's a world that the Bible begins by describing as good.[7]

Relationships entail choices too. Do we build or tear down? Do we honour or ignore? Do we work at a relationship or neglect it? Choices always have consequences and the consequences of living without reference to God are all around. We live in a fractured world together with the kind of shattered relationships graphically portrayed in Spielberg's film *The Color Purple*.

Jesus would say, 'It is that situation that I've come to rescue you from.' The perilously dangerous situation of living out of sync with God. A situation that ends every time with the same outcome: as the apostle Paul explains, 'the wages of sin is death'.[8] In other words, if you don't live the way that God intends it'll end up killing you.

Jesus' rescue was to offer life to people. And ironically (just like the crew of the spaceship *Messiah* in *Deep Impact*) it was through his death that he went about his rescue mission. Before explaining that, though, I think there are some facts that Jesus would want Steven Spielberg to know about real rescue.

'First, you don't have to earn it'.

As Tom Hanks's exhausted company pick their way through enemy territory on their mission to save Private Ryan, the eight-man party engage in a furious debate as to why one man's life is worth risking all of theirs. 'Ryan better be worth it,' Hanks says. 'He better go home and cure some disease or invent a new longer-lasting lightbulb.'

At the end of the film, fifty years on, Private Ryan visits the graves of the men who died to give him life. 'I lived my life the best I could,' he says to their gravestones. 'I hope in your eyes I've earned what you've done for me.' He's clearly stricken with guilt and doubt. Anguished, Ryan turns to his wife, looking for reassurance: 'Tell me I've led a good life.' he pleads, 'Tell me I'm a good man.'

'You are,' his wife responds. Her words feel utterly inadequate when faced with the gravestones of people who paid the ultimate price. It's clear no-one can repay such a debt.

Jesus would say, 'You don't have to and you can't. My rescue mission is not dependent on you paying for it in advance or in retrospect. You don't have to produce anything to prove you've been worth rescuing. You don't have to pay me back. That wouldn't be fair. That wouldn't even be possible.'

Jesus came to rescue us from our independence from God. Ironically, it's that same independence that so often prevents people from grabbing the lifeline, from being rescued. Despite all the evidence to the contrary, we still want to do it alone, climb out ourselves, or earn our way into God's good books.

Jesus would say to Steven Spielberg, 'Please understand, it cannot be done, not ever.' The reality is that the beast is within us too. We are not good people, but we don't need to be. The only qualification for rescue is that we recognize that we need it, that we're dying and that we can't help ourselves.

Secondly, I think Jesus would calm a nagging fear. 'Let me assure you there are no limits to who can be rescued.'

Perhaps Jesus would remind Spielberg of a scene in *Schindler's List*. A young woman pleads with Oskar Schindler to employ her ageing parents: 'They say that no-one dies here,' she says. 'They say that your factory's a haven. They say that you are good. I don't have any money. I borrowed these clothes. I'm begging you. Please, please bring them here.' At first Schindler angrily refuses, but later he relents.

Later in the film, Schindler approaches the Germans with a request to purchase concentration-camp prisoners for his factory. The scene shifts to a dingy office where he dictates to his factory manager the names of those he will buy. He pauses periodically and asks for a tally of names. Eventually, he stops, having reached his limit. The typist looks up: 'This list is life.'

At the end of the film, with the war just ended, Oskar Schindler falls to his knees in tears: 'I could have got more out. I could have got more out. If I'd made more money. I threw away so much money … I didn't do enough.'

Schindler rescued those he had encountered, those

who asked for help, those he met along the way. He had vast resources with which to purchase and protect these people. But they were finite resources. Schindler was painfully aware of the limits of his rescue mission. There were some he could not help.

Jesus would say to Steven Spielberg and to you, 'There are no limits to who I can rescue. You don't need an advocate to speak to me on your behalf. You don't need the right background or status. You don't even need to have been in contact with me before. There are no limits to my resources. Whoever comes to me, I will rescue.'

With that, Jesus would offer to Steven Spielberg the hope of a bright and certain future. 'Allow me to rescue you, to give you something that was hinted at when Schindler rescued so many Jews.'

At one point in the film, an administrative error sends a train filled with Jews to Auchswitz instead of the safety of Schindler's new factory. The morning after their late-night arrival, they are lined up and inspected by a camp commander. The tense silence is pierced by a single voice: 'Sir. A mistake has been made, we are not supposed to be here. We work for Oskar Schindler. We are Schindler Jews.'

The man from whom they take their name goes to Auchswitz in person and brings them to his home town. Now together, a crowd of men and women and children fills the factory floor. Oskar Schindler welcomes them personally. All known to him, individually named and rescued.

The Bible describes another list that is life. It contains the names of all those who have been rescued by Jesus. The Bible also describes a gathering of people. So vast that no-one will be able to count. Individuals all known by name and individually rescued. These are Jesus' people and he will be there in person, to welcome them home. They say no-one dies there. They say that it is a haven: God 'will wipe every tear from their eyes. There will be no more death or mourning or crying or pain.'[9]

God has intervened personally on our behalf. Jesus dying on a wooden cross is God's master image. It is God choosing to become the innocent victim. It is God standing in the line of fire. God, in the person of Jesus, willingly experiencing the consequences of our bad choices – making rescue a possibility.

The remaining question is the same as Private Ryan's. What is Spielberg's response to someone who paid the ultimate price? What is our response to a God who offers life by virtue of his death?

We all still have this choice because God still wants relationship. We can choose to turn around and ignore the rescuer. To try and make it alone, or simply to deny the danger. We can attempt to earn the rescuer's favour or even try and pay back the debt. Or we can humbly accept that we can't, and with gratitude take hold of the hand of the rescuer, who will take us out of the death zone and lead us home.

I'm in no doubt that Jesus would make his offer of rescue to Steven Spielberg as he does to you. The only unanswered question is: how does the last scene play out? What will you do with the hand of the rescuer?

8. What would Jesus say to Glenn Hoddle?

I have a degree of sympathy for Glenn Hoddle. There, I've said it. I can't agree with the sentiments that he expressed about the disabled and reincarnation. But to be hounded out of his job as England coach for expressing his religious beliefs – however offensive – is more than a little worrying. The press had a field day with Hoddle's 'nutty and medieval beliefs', presumably causing no little offence themselves to the millions of Hindus and Buddhists who believe in reincarnation.

Glenn Hoddle was considered by most to be one of the most talented footballers of his generation. It was big news when, following a trip with the England team to Israel, he was reported to have 'found God'. The comedian Jasper Carrott joked that it must have been some pass.

Glenn was widely described as a 'born-again Christian', a tag that he continues to attract in the press. Even in the aftermath of that controversial interview with *The Times* on 30 January 1999, when he made his comments about reincarnation and the disabled, papers still talked about him being a Christian. It's understandable; it's how he described himself in an interview that he gave a few days later. 'It's no secret that I am a Christian and I like to think that I care about people on quite a deep level.'[1]

Many years after his trip to Israel I was intrigued by an interview that Hoddle gave to the football magazine *Four Four Two* in which he asserted that it wasn't accurate to describe him as a born-again Christian.[2]

This was confirmed in a radio interview that Hoddle gave just before the 1998 World Cup, where he confirmed that while he had nothing personally against born-again Christians, he wouldn't describe himself as one. Instead he preferred to speak in terms of relating to God on what he described as a 'spirit level'.[3]

So Glenn seems to draw a distinction between Christians and born-again Christians. I think that this is something that a lot of people would agree with. For a long time I thought that born-again Christians were part of some sort of strange American cult. Things that I read in the papers made them seem strange and extreme. Whoever these people were, they were clearly very odd. So it came as a massive shock to me, many years later, to hear that Jesus used the phrase 'born again'. I didn't know much about the Bible, but this demanded further investigation.

The context of Jesus' statement is this: a member of the Jewish ruling council, Nicodemus, had come to see Jesus under the cover of night. He had some questions for Jesus, which he wanted to ask him quietly.

> 'Rabbi, we know you are a teacher who has come from God. For no-one could perform the miraculous signs you are doing if God were not with him.'
> In reply Jesus declared, 'I tell you the truth, no-one can see the kingdom of God unless he is born again.'[4]

It seems a strange reply, doesn't it? Jesus appears to answer a question that Nicodemus isn't asking. But in doing so he cuts to the very heart of the issue of how you can be right with God. Nicodemus has to be born again, or put another way, he has to undergo a spiritual rebirth. It's a condition of being in the kingdom of God. Christ says that to be one of his followers, to be a Christian, you have to be born again.

A Christian, then, by definition, has to be born again. There's no other sort. Maybe this is something that Jesus would want to clear up as he spoke to Glenn Hoddle. That any distinction between 'born-again' and 'ordinary' Christians is a false one.

Or perhaps Jesus would want to talk about reincarnation.

Although it was Hoddle's comments to *The Times* which caused all the controversy, in his radio interview on 17 May 1998 he also expressed his belief in reincarnation: 'I think we make mistakes when we are down here and our spirit has to come back and learn, that's why there is an injustice in the world, why there are certain people born into the world with terrible physical problems and why there is a family who have got everything right, physically and mentally.'[5] He also likened our physical bodies to an overcoat that is discarded when we die, with the spirit living on.

He expanded on these thoughts in *The Times*: 'You and I have been physically given two hands and two legs and half-decent brains. Some people have not been born like that for a reason. The karma is working from another lifetime. I have nothing to hide about that. It is not only people with disabilities. What you sow, you have to reap.'[6]

First off, we have to acknowledge that it isn't easy to stand up in a male sporting environment and talk about a belief in God. A lot of blokes seem to see religion as being for women and children. The fact that Glenn seems quite unfazed at talking about a faith in God is unusual, but good for him. He's happy to take the knocks from detractors and stand up for what he believes in. To comment that our main purpose in life is to learn spiritually, for instance, is a brave thing.

He's unashamed at being regarded as a spiritual man. He sees suffering around him, and like a lot of people is struggling to work out why, for instance, some people are born disabled while others are able-bodied.

In this spiritual search he has been influenced by Eileen Drewery, who describes herself as a spiritual healer. Initially sceptical, Hoddle reports coming back from injury after Eileen prayed for him while he was just a teenager. It was ten years later that he says the penny dropped and he understood more of what it was all about. As a result he understands the doubts that people have; for a decade he had a lot of the same questions too. From then on the former England coach encouraged his players to see Eileen for physical and mental healing.

Glenn even goes so far as to state that the biggest mistake that he made in France '98 was not taking her to the tournament from the very beginning.[7] She has gone on record as saying that 'Reincarnation is a belief that I hold and it may be something that is important to Glenn.'[8]

However, the doctrine of reincarnation isn't upheld in Christianity. And this is where you can understand people's confusion about Hoddle's beliefs. On the one hand Hoddle identifies himself as a Christian. On the other he talks about his belief in reincarnation, a belief that isn't Christian.

Jesus doesn't talk about reincarnation but about heaven and hell. He doesn't talk about a repeated cycle of lives, but one life, followed by judgment. It's an idea that we find throughout the Bible. Genesis talks of us being created from dust and returning to dust.[9] In addition to this the New Testament records that, 'Just as man is destined to die once, and after that to face judgment, so Christ was sacrificed once to take away the sins of many people.'[10]

The message of the Bible stands in contradiction to the idea of reincarnation. It's not a Christian doctrine. But this is by no means the only way in which Glenn Hoddle departs from orthodox Christianity.

You don't read *Glenn Hoddle: My 1998 World Cup Story* expecting detailed theological debate, but it does offer us further clues as to what Glenn believes. For instance he talks about having some faith in astrologers, something which again is at odds with the message of the Bible.[11] It's also interesting that while he talks about praying, he describes it in terms very different from the way that Jesus describes it.

Hoddle writes about walking out on to the pitch before the World Cup game against Tunisia: 'The first thing that I did out there was say a prayer. I did the same in Poland, and in Rome, and I would be doing it before every big game we played. It wasn't a prayer to win the game. It doesn't work like that. It's more like a positive vibration, asking for an energy to help overcome any negativity in the stadium.'[12]

Perhaps Jesus would talk to Glenn Hoddle concerning what prayer is all about, because if you take a look at the way that Jesus taught his followers to pray, it's clearly different. Listen to what he says when they ask him to explain it:

This, then, is how you should pray:

Our Father in heaven,
hallowed be your name,
your kingdom come,
your will be done

> on earth as it is in heaven.
> Give us today our daily bread.
> Forgive us our debts,
>   as we also have forgiven our debtors.
> And lead us not into temptation,
> but deliver us from the evil one.[13]

Jesus and Glenn Hoddle seem to have differing opinions about how you pray. Jesus seems to place the emphasis on depending on God as a Father and the business of forgiveness. It's hard to see how this is linked with stuff about positive vibrations and overcoming negativity.

So Jesus and Glenn Hoddle would probably talk about what a born-again Christian is, and reincarnation, and how we should pray. But that is not all. I think that Jesus would want to talk about something more important. Because during all the controversy about the England coach's sacking, I think we missed the most important issue.

In his World Cup diary, Glenn talks about the gift that Eileen Drewery claims to have:

> I know what she does but she will explain it herself in her own book. Her healing has had an effect on many different people – she was using her wonderful gift when I first met her when I was eighteen. She is so down to earth and uncomplicated. When she explains how she uses God's power through love she makes it all sound so simple. Look at Jesus. You didn't find him in the churches. He actually

challenged the churches of his day. His disciples were fishermen. He was a normal run-of-the-mill sort of guy who had a genuine gift, just as Eileen has got. God works through such people. Understanding how they work is an individual thing, a search within yourself for positive solutions and positive answers. Most people look for answers outside themselves, but the answers are on the inside. It doesn't matter if you are a pub landlord, a politician, or even royalty. We are all equal in God's eyes.[14]

There is much here that agrees with the Christian understanding of God. That Jesus challenged the religious authorities of his time is undeniable. That his disciples were drawn from all walks of life, some of them being fishermen, is another case in point. Many would also agree that just as Jesus healed many people, God is still in the business of healing. Christians would also want to agree strongly that God worked through Jesus, albeit sometimes in the synagogues that Jesus did attend.

But there is a fundamental sticking-point here, something that Christians can't agree with, that Jesus was 'a normal run-of-the-mill guy with a genuine gift'. This view of Jesus is filled out by how Hoddle explains his view of God. He uses the illustration of a wheel where God is the hub at the centre. The spokes running from the wheel's rim to its hub represent all the different religions. The idea is clear, that all religions lead to God.[15]

You can see why this is an attractive picture for many people. To relate to God without having to worry about institutional religion is an attractive thing for many. It might appeal to our individuality, or to our suspicion about religious institutions. Perhaps it seems a purer spirituality as a result.

It'd be an interesting discussion between Jesus and Glenn Hoddle. Because I think that the most important thing that Jesus would like to ask him is a question that he often asked those who followed him: 'Who do you think I am?'

Because although Christians believe that Jesus was a man, they also believe that he was a lot more than that. The truth is a lot more mind-blowing than any healing. It's the claim that Jesus made to be God in the flesh.

If the claim is true that Jesus is God in the flesh, we have to take it very seriously. If God in the flesh makes exclusive claims about how to know God, it puts the furore about reincarnation into the shade. The most important issue has to be who Jesus is rather than why there are some who are born with disability.

It might be surprising to you to find that there are dozens of ways that Jesus makes the claim to be God. For the sake of simplicity I want to concentrate on one of the titles that he used to describe himself, that of being Son of God. Perhaps Jesus would talk to Glenn about this one title, and explain what he meant by calling himself the Son of God. Because if Jesus is exclusively the Son of God, the quarrel about reincarnation is neither here nor there. More importantly, Jesus is saying something that many will find a great deal more offensive. He's saying that other teachers and gurus are leading their followers up a cul-de-sac.

Now the chances are that the phrase 'Son of God' has you scratching your head a little. Surely calling yourself the Son of God is different from claiming to be God himself? Let's see.

In the biography that John wrote of the life of Jesus, 'Son of God' is a title that he records being used of Jesus numerous times. In fact, right in the first chapter, John the Baptist calls Jesus the Son of God: 'I have seen and I testify that this is the Son of God.'[16]

And Jesus is recorded as claiming to be the Son of God on numerous occasions too. On one of those occasions Jesus heals a man who has been crippled for thirty-eight years. He gets into trouble for it. The Jewish authorities are upset that he heals the man on the Sabbath, the seventh day of the week that the Jews regarded as holy. John tells us that Jesus was persecuted for doing this. Notice how he makes his defence:

> Jesus said to them, 'My Father is always at his work to this very day, and I, too, am working.' For this reason the Jews tried all the harder to kill him; not only was he breaking the Sabbath, but he was even calling God his own Father, making himself equal with God.[17]

Because we live in a different time and culture

from those of this incident, we don't see the implications of what Jesus says here. But the Jews certainly did! Their reaction was to try to kill Jesus and we're even told why. In calling God his Father, Jesus was making himself equal with God. It's an astonishing claim. Far from using a different and distinct title, calling himself the Son of God made Jesus equal with God. It's a claim to be God.

It wasn't just a slip of the tongue, either. In a further debate with the Jews, Jesus also spells it out very clearly, so that there can be no misunderstanding what he says: 'I and the Father are one.'[18]

Again, if you read the reactions of the Jews who heard him you see that they wanted to stone him.

> ... but Jesus said to them, 'I have shown you many great miracles from the Father. For which of these do you stone me?'
>
> 'We are not stoning you for any of these,' replied the Jews, 'but for blasphemy, because you, a mere man, claim to be God.'[19]

There's not a lot of room for misunderstanding here, is there? The Jews knew that the way that Jesus called God his Father was a claim to be God. This outraged them because they couldn't accept that Jesus was other than a mere man – however amazing his gifts were. Glenn Hoddle seems to have the same difficulty in believing this.

It was a battle that went on for a long time. Wherever Jesus went, the Jewish religious leaders pursued him, plotting against him. They tried to trip him up with their questions, and when that failed they tried to kill him.

In the end the Jews got their way, or so it appeared. Jesus was betrayed by one of the men who had spent three years following him, and was then arrested, sentenced and put to death. Look at why he was crucified:

> The Jews insisted, 'We have a law, and according to that law he must die, because he claimed to be the Son of God.'[20]

It's a key question, this business of who Jesus is. Is he an ordinary run-of-the-mill bloke, albeit one with an extraordinary gift, as Hoddle says? Or is he something much more, the Son of God, as Jesus himself claimed so many times? So I think that this is the first question that Jesus would want to ask Glenn Hoddle: 'Who do you say I am?'

It's a question that you and I need to think about too.

But, hang on, we've already seen that when he was teaching his disciples how to pray, Jesus taught them to address God as Father. So what's the big deal about Jesus talking about the other side of the equation and calling himself Son of God? And if we are told by Jesus to address God as our Father, does that make us sons and daughters of God too?

Well, we are certainly invited to enjoy an intimate relationship with God. But let's look at some of the things that Jesus says in connection with being the Son of God. When we do, we see that Jesus' relationship with his Father is quite unlike any that we might enjoy with God. We've already seen something of this in the claims that Jesus made, perhaps most notably that Jesus and the Father are one.

This is made even more explicit in a couple of other places. First, there's an occasion where Jesus is arguing with the religious leaders and he makes the most stupendous claim: 'When a man believes in me, he does not believe in me only, but in the one who sent me. When he looks at me, he sees the one who sent me.'[21]

Those he was arguing with would have been outraged! Jesus claims to have been sent by God, and on top of that says that if you believe in him you believe in God, the one who sent him. Just to make sure that there's no misunderstanding here, he then asserts that if a person looks at him, he sees the one who sent him. If you look at Jesus you see God. You can never accuse Jesus of ducking the issue.

Then secondly, in a more relaxed setting, Jesus spends time making sure that the disciples know the truth about who he is: 'No-one comes to the Father except through me. If you really knew me, you would know my Father as well. From now on, you do know him and have seen him.'[22]

Well, that's some statement to start with! You can't come to God except through Jesus. In an age of tolerance, that goes down well and guarantees that you'll be popular! But look what Jesus goes on to tell the disciples: 'If you really knew me and who I am, you'd know God. You do know him; you've seen him.'

One of the disciples is still slow to catch on, or perhaps he is the only one brave enough to admit that he's confused. Either way, Philip says to him, 'Lord, show us the Father and that will be enough for us.' Perhaps he's frustrated with the riddles that he thinks Jesus is speaking in and just wants to get to the bottom of this mystery. 'Show us God and we'll be happy.'

Jesus answered: 'Don't you know me, Philip, even after I have been among you such a long time? Anyone who has seen me has seen the Father.'[23]

In talking this way, could Jesus have been any clearer about the uniquely close relationship that he had with the Father? To be able to say to Philip, 'You can stop wondering what God is like; you've met me already. If you've seen me, you've seen God.' This is either the most appalling arrogance, the worst of delusions, a terrible lie, or it's the truth.

The enormous claim that Jesus makes is to be God. Though we might be loath to admit it, there are times when virtually each one of us lies awake at night, turning over the big questions of life. Asking if there is a God. Wondering what such a God is like.

Jesus says, 'Look at me and see what God is like.'

Jesus would ask Glenn Hoddle, 'Who do you think I am?' because it's more than just an academic question. In his teaching Jesus stresses that a lot rests on this decision. 'Whoever believes in the Son has eternal life, but whoever rejects the Son will not see life.'[24] It's a matter of life and death. It's a question that faces each one of us too. Who do you say that he is?

9. What would Jesus say to Mulder and Scully?

The scene is a gloomy cave. It's eerily quiet. The silence is disturbed by the sound of tentative footsteps as someone tries to get a closer look at the remains of what was apparently here. A rock platform juts out from the wall, on it the remnants of what was present. There have been strange occurrences in the area – unusual geological episodes, figures of light, men running from the scene. The cave entrance darkens as someone else approaches. They peer inside, not daring to enter. Wondering whether to believe.

The harsh tones of a mobile phone pierce the silence and a man quickly answers: 'Scully, where are you? Get over here right away, I have something you must see.'

Special agents Fox Mulder and Dana Scully investigate cases involving possible paranormal phenomena, collectively known as the X-Files. First opened in 1946, the X-Files contain thousands of unexplained and unsolved cases. For nearly fifty years they remained ignored, incarcerated in the depths of FBI headquarters in Washington DC until Agent Mulder made them his life's work and obsession.

'Spooky' Mulder is an Oxford-educated psychologist. Working first in the FBI's Behavioural Science Unit, he made a name for himself when his psychological profiling helped catch an infamous serial killer. He is consumed by a passion to discover the truth about the X-Files, ignited when he witnessed what he believes was his sister's abduction by aliens.

Dana Scully was drafted on to the X-Files by Mulder's somewhat shady superiors and tasked with using her scientific expertise to debunk agent Mulder's work. In contrast to Mulder, Scully is a sceptic. A forensic doctor by training, science is her guiding light. She believes only in the hard facts and has a reputation for doing things by the book. But since her involvement in the X-Files Scully has seen things too. Things that her science struggles to explain.

Despite danger, despair and fierce opposition, Mulder and Scully relentlessly pursue the truth together. Their all-out search has led them into the realm of the fantastic and the dangerous. Challenging the very government that pays them, they consistently discover evidence of conspiracy and cover-up. Evidence that is mysteriously and sometimes violently withdrawn, just as it comes within reach.

Their search for truth and their different approaches would make an encounter with Jesus fascinating, not least because Jesus claimed to be the source of that for which Mulder and Scully both search. A revelation that Mulder once described as having 'greater implications for humankind than any other imaginable'.[1]

So what would Jesus say to Mulder and Scully? I think Jesus might start by saying, 'Mulder, Scully, you're right to search for the truth. Don't give up. Keep searching and you will find it. The truth is "out there" and can be discovered. It is even more staggering than you know.'

Jesus' quiet offer of help would seize Mulder and Scully's attention. 'To discover what truth is, look at me. "I am the truth."'[2]

Not the truth about extraterrestrial life, but the truth about life itself. The truth about people and the world and God. A God who made contact and offers us first-hand knowledge of that truth. It's that kind of knowledge that Jesus was offering. I think that Mulder might stop and listen to that.

The possibility of God turning up has got Mulder's attention once before. At the start of one *X-Files* episode, a man lies dying from a bullet wound. Another man enters the room, reaches down and touches the wound with the palm of his hand. The wound disappears. Mulder arrives on the scene to be told by the victim, 'God spared my life today.'[3]

That's the truth that Jesus would invite Mulder and Scully to investigate. The truth about God turning up to communicate with us in the only language we know. God putting on human clothes, coming into our world, showing extraordinary power, saying and doing extraordinary things – all for the good of others.

Mulder and Scully are sceptical of power. They are often the victims of its inappropriate use. But they're also drawn to the possibility of power being used for good and for truth – a hallmark of Jesus' life.

Mulder and Scully would be suspicious. After all they've experienced, who wouldn't be? The question they'd ask would be the same question they ask every week: 'How can we know this is the truth?' 'What can we trust to authenticate reality?' After all, someone claiming to be God isn't that unusual, it's happened in the X-Files! At the same time, such a claim would be irresistible to them, and they would certainly start to look for the clues. But the question remains, what authenticates Jesus' claim to be the truth?

Jesus would take that question seriously; he always did when it was sincerely asked. Jesus would say, 'Consider extreme possibilities. Scully, you're a scientist; I want you to weigh the evidence and decide on the results. Mulder, don't get carried away with your desire to believe; investigate carefully and then decide.'

That may surprise you. People often think that to be a Christian is to commit intellectual suicide. But you never see Jesus encouraging thoughtless conclusions. I don't know where the 'please leave your brain in the jar provided' idea of Christianity came from, but it certainly wasn't from Jesus.

One event can answer the 'True or false?' question about Jesus. If it happened it would make Jesus' claim to be God a sure-fire bet. If it didn't, the lie would be exposed and the Jesus File should be declared the biggest conspiracy of them all.

Jesus was executed for blasphemy: his claim to be God resulted in a plot to remove him. But Jesus seemed to know this was coming, and, more importantly, he talked about coming back again.

The scene at the start of this chapter could have been from many an *X-Files* episode. What it described was the scene that greeted those who first discovered that Jesus had disappeared. Of the body that had lain on the rock platform in a stone tomb, only the burial clothes were left. Could the extreme possibility have become reality? Like some of the X-Files, the claim might sound too amazing to be real. But stick with it. Extreme possibilities deserve careful consideration.

Jesus was publicly executed; his body was buried in a cave, which was secured with a one-ton boulder, authenticated by a government seal and guarded by special-service soldiers. Three days later, friends of Jesus who had come to anoint the body with perfume found the soldiers gone, the stone moved and the body missing. It's some mystery. How come the tomb was empty?

Mulder and Scully would no doubt suspect a conspiracy. Perhaps the Jewish authorities had stolen the body? The problem here, as they would discover, is the motive. After all, the Jews had spent considerable time and effort in removing Jesus. Would they really fuel belief in the God-man by making it look as if he'd made the ultimate comeback? If they had stolen the body, they would only have to produce it again to kill off the claims of his disciples that Jesus was alive.

But although the authorities didn't have the body, Mulder and Scully's suspicions of interference are well founded. Eyewitnesses report how the embarrassed priests and elders covered up by paying the soldiers guarding the tomb to say that the disciples of Jesus had stolen his body while they were asleep.[4] The Roman soldiers were understandably uncomfortable with this version of events as sleep on duty meant death afterwards! Those offering the bribe promised to take care of their superiors. What they failed to take care of was the flaw in their argument. If the guards were sleeping, how did they know it was the disciples that stole the body?

As the possibility of the unbelievable grows, I can imagine Mulder becoming more and more intrigued and Scully becoming even more determined to find a scientific explanation. Time and again Scully has made a critical breakthrough by studying the medical evidence. Hours spent in the lab have frequently shed light on some very dark cases.

Perhaps Jesus wasn't really dead. After all, Scully has seen comatose states that resemble death before. Could Jesus have been another? His recovery in the tomb would explain the missing body and his 'after-death appearances'.

Yet, Jesus was executed by experts who were paid to get it right! The Romans required several experts to confirm the victim's death. And crucially, the evidence of eyewitnesses deals a fatal blow to the coma theory. John's account of the death of Jesus puts it like this:

> But when they [the soldiers] came to Jesus and found that he was already dead, they did not break his legs [usually done to finish the victim off]. Instead, one of the soldiers pierced Jesus' side with a spear, bringing a sudden flow of blood and water.[5]

Scully's medical expertise would both make sense of this and confound her. Here was medical evidence that supported the account of Jesus' crucifixion. The spear had pierced both the pericardial sac surrounding the heart (releasing water-like serum) and the heart itself (hence the sudden flow of blood). Such an injury is not survivable. The conclusion is inescapable. If Jesus was alive again, he was not back from a coma; he was back from the cold.

Within days of Jesus' death, Jerusalem was buzzing with talk of him being seen. Not an isolated incident, but ten separate occasions, involving hundreds of people, which history records. If we're finally to put Jesus to rest, we must adequately explain these.

It's a well-documented fact that people devastated by grief sometimes claim to see those they have lost. Naturally, Scully might be tempted to point to such hallucinations as the rational explanation for a seemingly paranormal phenomenon. Obviously, Jesus' followers were quite naturally swept away in a tide of grief. They were simply suffering from hallucinations due to emotional trauma.

This time, and somewhat unusually, Mulder could provide the necessary objectivity by virtue of his psychological training. He'd be pleased to turn the scientific tables on his partner, with a wry 'That's good, Scully, but what you're forgetting is that hallucinations obey certain observable scientific rules.'

First, they are confined to certain psychological types, people with particular mental illnesses or those prone to severe emotional instability. The likelihood that all those who claimed to see Jesus suffered in this way is, to say the least, small. Those who saw him were ordinary people, from different backgrounds and places.

Secondly, hallucinations of this kind usually relate to an event that is probable or at least hoped for. Most of Jesus' followers hid after his death, fearing that they would be next to be executed in this way. Meanwhile, Mary and the other women went to the tomb to take care of a corpse, which is hardly the behaviour of those expecting his imminent reappearance.

Hallucinations tend to occur in 'likely surroundings' such as the home of the deceased. Jesus was seen on a mountain, by a lake, in an upstairs room and on a country road. Hallucinations are normally seen over a long period of time, either gradually fading or increasing to a point of mental breakdown. Yet sightings of Jesus happened over a forty-day period and then stopped, all at once.

Finally, the probability against two individuals hallucinating the same thing is astronomical. Paul, an early church leader, tells how more than five hundred people saw Jesus at the same time. So confident was he of what they'd seen that he invited his readers to go and check it out for themselves as most of these people were still alive.[6]

I'm sure that Scully, presented with that weight of evidence, would conclude that hallucinations cannot account for Jesus' post-death appearances. Put together with the rest of the evidence, the most reasonable explanation for what happened, then and since, is that the Truth could not be killed. Jesus did rise from the dead, the only man ever to fight the future and win.

Jesus' appearances turned people's lives around. The same disciples who had fled the city and later locked themselves away in a secret hideaway were within days fearlessly declaring Jesus to be alive and well. As they travelled to tell people about Jesus, they were often beaten and imprisoned. In time most were killed, all because they would not stop telling people that Jesus was alive.

Even people as sceptical as Scully were convinced. Thomas was a close friend and follower of Jesus and believed only in the hard facts. When his ecstatic friends told him that Jesus was back, he refused to believe unless he could see for himself. He wanted hard proof. 'Unless I see the nail marks in his hands and put my finger where the nails were, and put my hand into his side, I will not believe it.'[7]

And Jesus did turn up with the proof in his hands:

A week later his disciples were in the house

again, and Thomas was with them ... Jesus came and stood among them and said, 'Peace be with you!' Then he said to Thomas, 'Put your finger here; see my hands. Reach out your hand and put it into my side. Stop doubting and believe.'

Thomas said to him, 'My Lord and my God!'[8]

Thomas touched the Truth and the man who is famous for his doubts believed.

Changed lives are still the enduring evidence of Jesus' ultimate comeback.

The 'so obvious it could be missed' implication of Jesus' resurrection is that he is alive today. The Truth can still be encountered because the person who is the Truth is alive.

I met Belinda on a camp several years ago. She looked like she was having a ball. But one evening she unloaded her desperation. She'd experienced the devastation of her family disintegrating and had gone on a search for love. She went from one encounter to the next – physically close but emotionally isolated. She eventually found security in the arms of an older man and with tears in her eyes told me how she'd trusted him and how he had abused her trust. Alone and desperate, she sought comfort in a bottle. She was seventeen.

Belinda had heard about Jesus. She'd seen the difference he made to others. She was naturally sceptical but knew she needed someone to trust. She'd thought long and hard and, sitting next to a lake, she asked Jesus to make the change for her.

Mulder and Scully have discovered time and again the pain and disappointment of being let down by those they should have been able to count on. In different circumstances so had Belinda. 'Trust no-one', the words with which Chris Carter, the show's creator, signs autographs, is a motto that lives beyond the *X-Files*.

That is where I think Jesus would leave Mulder and Scully. He'd make the same offer to them as he did to Thomas and others he met. The same offer he is still making today. Jesus would say, 'The Truth can be trusted. Trust me.'

Time and again he invited people to put their trust in him, not to acknowledge his existence mentally but to put something of theirs in his hand: themselves.

When Belinda tentatively trusted Jesus, the Truth met her. The next day, her friends were asking what had happened. She displayed an almost tangible serenity, in stark contrast to the struggle and anguish of the previous months. Most of her problems hadn't gone anywhere. But she'd met the one person who could be totally trusted. Who had shown her that by showing up. And who promises never to leave. She now knew the Truth, the Truth who had her best interests at heart and the power to make the difference. She knew that she would never be the same.

In episode 82517, Mulder asks Scully why she refuses to believe. Scully replies: 'I just need more than you. I need proof.'

Jesus would say to Mulder and Scully and to you:

'Trust the Truth.' Consider the evidence and then move towards it. It's at that point that you'll meet the truth. You'll find the proof you are looking for. You'll experience the certainty of Thomas and Belinda and countless others. By all means look at it carefully, painstakingly. But there comes a time when you must make up your mind.

The evidence for the resurrection of Jesus is hard to dismiss. If you can't accept the resurrection, the onus is on you to come up with a better explanation. If he did rise from the dead, it validates the special claims he made about himself. It's a mind-blowing possibility.

As Mulder says in an episode of the *X-Files*, enthusing to Scully about the authenticity of an extraterrestrial biological entity, 'Proof would change everything. Every truth we live by would be shaken to the ground. There is no greater revelation imaginable.'

10. What would Jesus say to Ben Elton?

I want to tell you something that you might find slightly distressing from a church minister. I have always loved Ben Elton's work. As well as seeing a lot of his work on TV and reading the novels, I've seen his stand-up routine a couple of times too. I think he's incredibly good at what he does; he's articulate and he's a thinker. He isn't afraid to stand out or to speak out. So many of his observations are spot on and – helpfully for a comedian – he's very, very funny. I would dearly love to have half his ability to communicate.

I had always suspected that aside from some of the bad language that he uses there was a strong moral undercurrent to his work. This was obvious from his environmental and political concerns, and when he wrote *Popcorn* it was no surprise to find that the book was intelligent and dealt with a variety of ideas. It looked like *Batman Forever* producer Joel

Schumacher might make it the first of his books to become a Hollywood film, though sadly it wasn't to be. What was perhaps more surprising was that the book dealt with sex and violence in films and is said to have won praise from Mary Whitehouse.

Popcorn deals with an issue that we are all very familiar with. It's the issue of our personal responsibility. We've all done it. Been caught in the wrong, failed to meet a deadline, and our first reaction is to own up? Not on your life! Our automatic reaction is to find someone to point the finger at. 'It's his fault.' 'She made me do it.'

The first thing that I think Jesus would say to Ben Elton is that he's dead right, this is the universal reaction we all have when someone points out our shortcomings. I think Jesus would point to the first man and woman and confirm it from the book of Genesis. Adam and Eve are allowed to eat the fruit from any tree in the garden – except one. No prizes for guessing what they do. Like most of us they want to try the forbidden fruit. Later God confronts them and wants to know why they have disobeyed him. Adam turns round and blames his wife – it was her fault. Eve in turn blames the serpent.[1] (And, as the old joke goes, the serpent that tempted them into trying the fruit in the first place didn't have a leg to stand on.)

We're all like that, aren't we? We like to be able to blame someone for the things that go wrong in our lives. It's the fault of our parents, our teachers, the government, our partner, the media, our genes, maybe even God. But it isn't my fault.

Most of the time we're blaming other people for fairly minor stuff. That isn't the case in *Popcorn*. Bruce Delamitri is a film director who has just won the Oscar for best director. It's a controversial choice because his film is a very violent one. Fifty-seven people die in it, and there are protest groups out claiming that his films are a bad influence on society. There are even fears that the film will encourage copycat killings.

He celebrates his win at the Governor's Ball, the big post-Oscars party. Bruce isn't a man who is slow in coming forward with his opinions; he's happy to speak his mind, and after a few drinks he does just that. He vents his fury at the victim-culture that he finds himself in, where no-one ever takes responsibility for his or her shortcomings.

> Nothing is anybody's fault. We don't do wrong, we have problems. We're victims, alcoholics, sexaholics. Do you know you can be a shopaholic? That's right. People aren't greedy any more, oh no. They're shopaholics, victims of commercialism. Victims! People don't fail any more. They experience negative success. We are building a culture of gutless, spineless, self-righteous, whining cry-babies who have an excuse for everything and take responsibility for nothing ...[2]

As if to illustrate his point, while all this is going on Wayne and his girlfriend Scout are watching films on video. And they're looking for someone to blame.

'I'm sick of watching the tube, honey,' the girl said.

'Quiet now, baby,' the man replied. This is important. What I'm doing here right now, hon, is researching.'

'Researching what? You ain't doing no researching. You're just watching dumb movies which you seen a hundred times already. I want to go out.'

'What I am researching, sugar,' the man said, his tone hardening slightly, 'is our salvation. Y'hear me now? Because what I have here is a plan to get us saved. You want to be saved, don't you, precious?'

'Sure I want to be saved. Everybody wants to be saved.'[3]

You see, Wayne and Scout are mass murderers. They're trying to find someone to blame for the murders that they've committed. Their plan of salvation is to pin the blame on a film director. They decide that Bruce Delamitri – this Quentin Tarrantino figure who makes violent and controversial films – is their best bet. Their plan of salvation is to blame him for what they've done. They want to say that the violent films of Bruce Delamitri influenced them, and so it wasn't their fault that they killed all these people.

So on the night of the Oscars, Bruce returns to his house to find that he has a couple of visitors. Wayne and Scout have broken in and they proceed to hold him hostage. All they want from him is the admission that the murders were all his fault.

What might Jesus say about all this?

We've already said that he'd recognize the behaviour all right. Having lived as a man among people for thirty-three years, even nearly 2,000 years ago, he'd recognize that character trait we have, of wanting to find someone else to blame, as being timeless.

And he'd want to say to Ben Elton, you're absolutely right about the fact that we're all, every single one of us, the whole human race, guilty. None of us lives life the way that we should. And none of us feels very comfortable in admitting to that or taking responsibility for it.

You see, whether he realizes it or not, Ben Elton has stumbled upon the heart of the Christian message.

Jesus would want to say, 'You're right, you're guilty.' None of us are as good as we should be, none of us lives up to the sort of standards that we should. Very few of us live up to the kinds of standards that we set for ourselves, not if we're honest. No-one, not one person on the whole of the planet, measures up to the standards that God has set for us. Because God is perfect, and none of us is. And because we're all guilty, we're facing punishment, just as Wayne and Scout are in the novel.

We know that because we're only human we make mistakes, and will never live the perfect life. If God's standards are perfection we haven't a chance. So we set our sights a lot lower than that and tell ourselves that if we're better than other people we'll be all right. Perhaps, if we can be good people and end up in the top half of humanity when we're all ranked at the end of our lives, we'll be OK. We'll get to heaven. Or perhaps we can be in the top quarter, perhaps that will be enough.

We aren't sure what the pass mark will be, but we'll try hard and hope for the best. We may not be Mother Teresa, but we're a lot better than Stalin or Hitler. We're generally all right. And when we aren't it's because of other people. So long as I measure up against other people I should be OK.

In his role as a writer on *The Young Ones*, Ben dealt with the adventures of four hapless students. There's a great bit in one of the episodes where the guys finally get their exam results. How have they done? Lenny Henry comes along playing the postman and brings them their letters and the devastating news that they have come bottom. Bottom in the whole world.

The way that they react to this news is brilliantly observed. Because what's the first thing that they ask? 'Who came top out of us?' They have failed in the most spectacular fashion, but forget that; how have they done compared to their friends?

Aren't we like that? So what if I've made mistakes in life? So I'm not as good as I should be; at least I'm better than some other people I could name! At least I'm better than she is. I'm not half as bad as him.

Jesus told a story that warns us against doing that: 'Two men went up to the Temple to pray, one a Pharisee, the other a tax man.'[4]

The Pharisees were a respected group of people in

the society that Jesus was in. They were the religious leaders of the Jews. They were looked up to.

In contrast, the tax man. Well, some things never change. This tax man was much more unpopular than his modern-day counterpart. Because he was a traitor. He was collecting taxes for the Romans, who were the occupying power. Imagine how unpopular a French mayor toadying up to the Nazis in the Second World War would be and you get some idea of how the Jews felt about the tax collectors. They also had a reputation for making a good amount of money on top of the quota that the Romans required.

The prayer of the Pharisee is very telling:

> The Pharisee posed and prayed like this: 'Oh, God, I thank you that I am not like other people – robbers, crooks, adulterers, or, heaven forbid, like this tax man. I fast twice a week and tithe on all my income.'[5]

Do you see the substance of his prayer? It starts with a list of the things that he isn't. He's doing well; he isn't a robber, crook or adulterer. Those are the bad things that he doesn't do.

Then there are the good things that he does. He fasted twice a week even though the law required him to fast only once – a year! No wonder people look up to him and admire his religious devotions. He gives away a tenth of everything he gets, again doing much more than the law requires.

And thirdly, the Pharisee compares himself with the tax man and says to God, 'I'm not like him! Look how good I am compared to him.' He's taken a look around, and compared himself to those he sees. And he reckons he's doing all right.

The Pharisee is right; he is nothing like the tax collector. The tax collector is humble and aware of the ways that he's made a mess of his life, in a way that doesn't even occur to the Pharisee. 'Meanwhile the tax man, slumped in the shadows, his face in his hands, not daring to look up, said, "God, give mercy. Forgive me, a sinner."'[6]

What does Jesus say about this? Here's the punchline: 'This tax man, not the other, went home made right with God.'[7]

As we read the story today we realize that, whether we're religious or not, we're just like that Pharisee. We think that the mental lists we make of the bad things that we avoid, and the good things that we do, will be enough. Or we take a look around and decide that we aren't doing too badly compared with some people. But look what Jesus says about the Pharisee that we resemble. He wasn't right with God as he left the temple that day.

This is heavy stuff, isn't it? It isn't a popular message, but it's one that Jesus tells us is the big problem as far as being a human being is concerned. We're all of us guilty, and all either comparing ourselves favourably with other people or looking for someone else to take the blame.

And Jesus would want to say to Ben Elton, and to you and me, that it doesn't have to be that way. This is the amazing part. Jesus would recognize what Ben Elton is talking about when he describes looking for a way out as a plan of salvation. He'd say, 'I know all about plans of salvation. I have one. It's very simple. You can stop looking for other people to blame, because I've already taken the blame for you.'

That's the incredible fact at the very centre of Christianity. Without it we might as well all pack up and go home. Jesus took the blame for you and me.

He knew that we'd never be good enough to get into heaven by our own efforts. God's perfect standards aren't possible; we're flawed and can't reach that level of perfection. The standards are there as a vivid reminder of how far short we fall. They're there to remind us that we've failed, that we can't get into God's good books through being good or going to church. The tax collector in the story recognized that and wasn't even able to lift his head. He just knew that he needed mercy. He knew that he was a sinner. That he'd made mistakes. That he didn't measure up to God's standards.

So it's good news for the tax collector that God does have a plan of salvation. God knew that we don't live lives that measure up, and that we've lost any kind of relationship with God as a result. Jesus took the blame and the punishment for us. He took the punishment once and for all when he died in our place, taking the punishment we deserve, crucified on a wooden cross.

Because Jesus took the blame and took the punishment for us, we can be forgiven and live new lives – in a relationship with God. It's an offer Jesus makes to each one of us. Jesus would say to Ben

Elton, and to you, 'You can be forgiven; you can live in a relationship with the God who made you.'

That leaves us with a decision to make. We have to respond to that offer. Do we accept what's on offer? Or do we reject it? There's no sitting on the fence; that's the equivalent of rejecting the offer. If we go to the supermarket and see a free offer we have to decide whether or not to accept it. There are only two options; it has to be yes or no. The only way to get the free gift is by deciding, 'Yes, I do want this.' You can't hang around near the checkouts hoping that something will somehow rub off and that you'll get the gift.

You don't become a Christian without making a decision and telling God that you want to live life with him. You won't get this priceless gift that's on offer, of a new life lived with God, with all your mistakes wiped out and forgiven, by hanging around in a church and doing the religious thing. Jesus made that clear in the story of the Pharisee and the tax man. You need to tell God that you want that gift, that you want to live life with him from now on.

In a nutshell, then, there it is. The most important decision any of us could ever make. I think Jesus would tell Ben Elton that he knows about plans of salvation, and that his is the original. I think he'd ask him to think about how he'd respond to that plan too.

11. What would Jesus say to Billy Graham?

For most of us, the thought of getting up and giving any sort of speech or talk is one that fills us with fear and trembling. Whether it's at a wedding or at a party to mark someone's leaving, it's the sort of thing that most of us would rather someone else did.

In his autobiography, Billy Graham reveals that as a boy he had no desire to become an evangelist, someone who spent his time explaining to people what Christianity was all about. For a start he was less than convinced about the Christians that he knew, regarding the noise from a prayer meeting held on his father's land as being made by 'some fanatics'.[1]

When the chance came to hear a Christian speak in his native Charlotte, the sixteen-year-old Graham decided that he didn't want anything to do with anyone called an evangelist, and declared to his parents that he wasn't going to hear him.[2] But Billy did go to the meetings, partly drawn out of curiosity because the evangelist had the reputation of being something of a fighter. What happened at those meetings was to turn his life around completely. We'll come back to that in more detail later.

After his conversion, Billy got to speak about his faith for the first time. He was asked to describe to a group of prisoners what it was like to be a Christian. He had no prior warning whatsoever.

> I tried, with my knees knocking. The ten or so prisoners looked off into the distance or picked their teeth for the two or three minutes I spoke ... It was the first public utterance I had given of my faith, but it reinforced my conviction that I would never become a preacher.[3]

Since then he's probably preached to more people than anyone else on the planet! The statistics are almost impossible to get your head round. The interviewer David Frost calculates that Billy has preached to 210 million people in 185 countries during his time.[4] Since then Billy has preached on the Internet, offering people all around the world the opportunity to hear the Christian message as he preached it during his campaign in Tampa, in October 1998.

Not bad for the son of a dairy farmer who confesses that after preaching, 'Almost every night I say, "I wish I had done much better ... "'[5]

Who knows how many people have responded to the message that Billy Graham has preached? It's impossible to put a figure to it. But clearly Billy Graham has been tremendously effective in what he does.

Asking the question 'What would Jesus say to Billy Graham?' seems almost fatuous, doesn't it? Surely Jesus would welcome him with open arms and thank him after all the tremendous work that Billy Graham has done for the cause of Christianity? Here's a man who worked hard and advanced the Christian gospel far beyond perhaps any other. Who preached and spoke to millions. Of course Jesus is going to be full of praise for him. The gates of the heaven that Billy preaches about are bound to swing open to welcome such a hard-working and successful evangelist, aren't they?

Well, actually, I don't think we want to be too quick to jump to that conclusion.

Jesus was always saying the unexpected and he challenged the way people thought about big issues like heaven and hell. Jesus spoke words that pull us up short and make us reconsider our attitude to heaven and how we get there.

In one example of this, Jesus warned people that not all prophets were true prophets. Some are actually wolves in sheep's clothing, bad guys masquerading as good. Jesus goes on to warn, 'Not everyone who says to me, "Lord, Lord," will enter the kingdom of heaven, but only he who does the will of my Father who is in heaven. Many will say to me on that day, "Lord, Lord, did we not prophesy in your name, and in your name drive out demons and perform many miracles?" Then I will tell them plainly, "I never knew you. Away from me, you evil doers!"⁶

Can you imagine the effect that this message must have had on those who heard Jesus? How could you ever know if you were going to heaven if some of the people who had done the most amazing things in the name of God were going to be turned away from the gates of heaven?

These people had impressive credentials, driving out demons and performing miracles. Still, that wasn't enough. Jesus says that he'll tell some with those qualifications that he never even knew them.

This is disturbing, isn't it? It means that none of us, not even the Reverend Billy Graham, can rely with any certainty on their great acts to win them a place in heaven. And if that's the case, we can't guarantee that Jesus would be welcoming Billy Graham with open arms when they meet.

Perhaps there's a crumb of hope in something that Jesus says when he's discussing true and false prophets. He gives us a way of working out who the wolves in sheep's clothing are. He tells us that you can recognize them by their fruits.⁷

In other words, you'll be able to work out who the true prophets are from the way that they behave, the things they say and the things they do. The way they live their lives. If they are habitually greedy for money, or violent, or have sexual affairs, for instance, you know that these aren't true prophets. Certainly nobody is perfect, and look closely enough at any of us and you'll find some flaws and some mistakes. But if the walk and the talk don't match up, Jesus warns us that the prophet or priest or evangelist is in terrible danger of being rejected at the end of the day.

Well, you look at the life of Billy Graham and I don't think you can fail to be impressed. He's made some mistakes in his time; he's the first to admit that. Being uncommitted wasn't one of them. To read his own account of the fifty years that he has spent travelling the world – and visiting every country in it – you can hardly fail to be struck by the energy and commitment of the man.[8] You read of some of the hard work that he has done and seriously wonder how he maintained the pace and still kept his sanity.

The meetings that he took in London in 1954, for instance, were initially attacked by the press and even by some in the church – bishops included. At the first meeting of a planned six-week campaign, it initially appeared that there would be more press than public in the meeting. Yet due to overwhelming public demand, the six weeks became twelve. Most of the talks that he gave were written on the day that they were delivered. It was a gruelling schedule and in the three months that he was in England for the campaign, Billy lost 30 lbs in weight.

In New York in 1957, a campaign that Billy believes physically took something out of him that would never be replaced, he recalls:

> I often spoke three or four times a day in addition to the Crusade service in the evening – perhaps a luncheon with business leaders, a visit to a university, a meeting at the United Nations, a gathering in someone's home

designed to reach out to neighbours or friends ... opportunities seemed limitless.⁹

Surely the sheer effort that he's put in must be enough to ensure that Billy Graham enters the heaven that he talks about so much? When you add his other qualities, doesn't the argument become even more irresistible?

In addition to this you have to be impressed by the integrity of the man. The life of an international evangelist must be fraught with pressures. Some in his position have fallen to sexual temptations; others have been found to have taken millions of dollars from those who thought they were supporting the work.

Knowing that these temptations could blow the work that he was engaged in out of the water, Billy has been wise on his travels. He is said to ensure that he never enters a hotel room alone, and he even makes it a rule never to 'travel, meet or eat alone with a woman other than my wife'.¹⁰ He's well aware of the need to be squeaky clean, for fear of the whole message that he preaches being brought into disgrace.

Right at the beginning of his ministry, way back in 1948, Billy realized that the amount of money that was being raised in the collections at his meetings could become a real problem. He knew that people would see the amounts collected and putting two and two together assume that he was in it for the money. He was also aware that there is a temptation for someone in his position to manipulate his audiences emotionally regarding the collection that was taken up in the meetings. So as early as 1948 he resolved to downplay the offering that they took up in the meetings and to avoid all financial abuses.

Even then the press still questioned his lifestyle. Billy was asked at a press conference in 1954 about the cost of him arriving by boat on the luxurious *Queen Mary* to come to Britain. Why didn't he travel like Jesus did? Graham replied, 'Well, Jesus travelled on a donkey; you find me a donkey that can swim the Atlantic, and I'll try to buy him.'[11]

I think that one of the things that endears Billy to people is the fact that they recognize him as a man of integrity. Not everyone will agree with the message he preaches, but it's very hard to dismiss him as just another televangelist.

So when we look at the fruit of his life, the way that he lives – in so far as we can ever judge – it begins to look more hopeful for Billy Graham. He seems to be a man who has lived a good life, and he's done a lot of good work for God. It looks like he's going to heaven, doesn't it?

Well, again, not necessarily. Again it might sound shocking to you, but living a good life, on top of doing a lot of work for God, does not guarantee that you'll make it. You might think that it's a disgrace that I could ever throw doubt on the issue. But consider this: Billy Graham would say the same thing himself.

Don't believe me? Well, listen to an answer that he gives to David Frost in an interview that Billy did with him in 1993. Frost puts it to him, 'You're obviously going to heaven, aren't you?'

> Billy Graham: Well, I'm going to heaven, not on my good works, or because I've preached to all those people or read the Bible. I'm going to heaven because of what Christ did on the cross.[12]

It's an incredible thought, isn't it? I'm sure God must love the work that Billy Graham does. God has used him massively in the work that he's done. And yet when they meet on judgment day, Billy Graham won't be able to say, 'Let me into your kingdom because of what I've spent my life doing.' It's only because of the business of Jesus being crucified that Billy Graham will get into the kingdom of heaven.

You might have thought that there was no way that anyone could ever be sure that they could be made right with God. If you can't be sure on the basis that you've lived a good moral life, or because you have faithfully worked for God, clearly you can never be sure of going to heaven.

Wrong. Billy outlines that he can be sure of going to heaven. And it's not through anything that he has done. The many achievements that he has to look back on aren't credentials that he can wave in the face of God. No, the only way that Billy Graham, or any one of us, can be put right with God is through responding to this message of the cross that Billy has devoted his life to preaching.

It's a message that he has repeated over and over to the millions who have come to hear him. Sure, the subjects talked about and the stories he tells are different, but the essential message remains unchanged.

One man attended all ninety-three meetings of one campaign and commented, 'I have only heard one message.'[13] Billy took it as a compliment!

What is that message? Billy outlines it at the very end of his autobiography.

> The message is, first of all, a message about God ... He created us and loves us so that we may live in harmony and fellowship with him. We are not here by chance.
>
> The message is also about the human race, and about each one of us. The Bible says that we have been separated and alienated from God because we have wilfully turned our backs on him and are determined to live our lives without him. This is what the Bible means by sin – choosing our way instead of God's way ... The evidence of this is all around us ... the headlines scream every day that we live in a broken, sin-ravaged world.
>
> But in addition, the message declares that God still loves us. He yearns to forgive us and bring us back to himself. He wants to fill our lives with meaning and purpose right now. Then he wants us to spend all eternity with him in heaven, free forever from the pain and sorrow and death of this world.
>
> Moreover, God has done everything possible to reconcile us to himself. He did this in a way that staggers our imagination. In God's plan, by his death on the cross, Jesus Christ paid the penalty for our sins, taking the

judgement of God that we deserve upon himself when he died on the cross. Now, by his resurrection from the dead, Christ has broken the bonds of death and opened the way to eternal life for us.

The resurrection also confirms for all time that Jesus was in fact who he said he was: the unique Son of God, sent from heaven to save us from our sins. Now God freely offers us the gift of forgiveness and eternal life.[14]

Perhaps you've wondered what Christianity was all about and never heard it explained so clearly and concisely before. It isn't, as is often thought, about being a good person and doing what you can for God and the people around you. It's no good relying on church attendance or working hard for the community.

It's about the opposite of thinking that you can do it by virtue of your virtue. Instead you need to realize that according to God's standards you aren't that great. At its most basic it's the challenge to stop living without God and start living with him in your life.

How can you do that?

This offer that God makes of forgiveness is one that needs to be responded to. As with any gift, we can accept it, unwrap it and enjoy it, or refuse it. There's no sitting on the fence on this one – if we say we'll think about the offer of the gift some other time, we haven't accepted the gift!

Accepting the gift isn't difficult, but it does have massive consequences. If you've never done it before, this is what you need to do.

First, you need to realize that there's a problem. Own up to the fact that you have lived your life without God as the centre of it. It's a blow to our pride to admit that we haven't come up to scratch and that we need to acknowledge the mistakes we've made.

Secondly, you need to believe there's a solution to that problem. You know that you can't put it right yourself – look at how unsuccessful your New Year's resolutions are. Put your trust in the offer that God makes – the message that Billy outlines. You can't be put right with God if you can't accept that God has done something about putting the problem right.

Finally, you need to put it into practice and accept the gift of forgiveness that's on offer. Pray. Tell God in your own words that you have lived without him, but that you're sorry, that you want to change, and ask him for his help in that. Jesus used the word 'repent' in talking to people – it means more than feeling sorry for the things that you do, but to actively turn right around, do a U-turn and start heading in the opposite direction. A part of that will be to get involved in a church; if you're serious about this U-turn you'll need the help of like-minded people.

Three simple steps that have giant consequences. This is the way to be put right with God. This is the way to start living a brand-new life.

What would Jesus say to Billy Graham? I'm sure he's pleased with the work that the evangelist has done for God. I'm sure that he'll be welcomed by

Jesus to enjoy eternity in heaven. But it isn't down to any of Billy's great qualities that he'll get there. It's simply because around his sixteenth birthday Billy responded to this message himself, after going to hear the preacher in Charlotte he'd vowed to avoid!

And Billy Graham knows that

> No matter who we are or what we have done, we are saved only because of what Christ has done for us. I will not go to heaven because I have preached to great crowds. I will go to heaven for one reason: Jesus Christ died for me, and I am trusting him alone for my salvation. Christ died for you also, and he freely offers you the gift of eternal life as you commit your life to him.[15]

If someone like Billy Graham can't get there by his own efforts, I figure that the rest of us are in trouble. If he's right about the only way to heaven being to trust Jesus, we all need to take that very seriously.

12. What would Jesus say to you?

It's interesting to consider what Jesus would say to the rich and the famous. But if you read any of the accounts of his life, you'll see that Jesus didn't spend great amounts of time with the style leaders of society. Instead he seemed to spend the vast majority of his time with ordinary men and women. People like you and me. Do you ever wonder what Jesus would have to say to you?

To start with, I think he'd want to urge you to take nothing that you've read so far in this book on the word of the people who wrote it. It's much more important that you check it out for yourself. Read one of those accounts of the life of Jesus. Read the stories that Jesus told. Read what he teaches. Many people do this and find that the words of Jesus speak to them today. They know what Jesus says to them as his words ring down through the ages. Those words still inspire, hitting home to us with fresh insight, as Jesus continues to teach us about ourselves.

I want to look at a warning that Jesus gives in his teaching. Issuing a warning might not be how you think of gentle Jesus. But if you read an account of Jesus' life you'll see that he often issues warnings. In the same way that a concerned parent might warn a child not to play with the fire, Jesus warns us not to do things that will cause us harm, and to do the things that will do us good. That's the reason behind everything that Jesus ever does; he wants the best for each of us.

With that in mind, let's look at the warning that Jesus issued to those who listened to him. It's a warning issued to all those who listen, whether they are famous or not. It's just as relevant to you and me as to any of the other figures that we've looked at.

> Then Jesus went through the towns and villages, teaching as he made his way to Jerusalem. Someone asked him, 'Lord, are only a few people going to be saved?'
>
> He said to them, 'Make every effort to enter through the narrow door, because many, I tell you, will try to enter and will not be able to. Once the owner of the house gets up and closes the door, you will stand outside knocking and pleading, "Sir, open the door for us."
>
> 'But he will answer, "I don't know you or where you come from."
>
> 'Then you will say, "We ate and drank with you, and you taught in our streets."

> 'But he will reply, "I don't know you or where you come from. Away from me, all you evildoers!"
>
> 'There will be weeping there, and gnashing of teeth, when you see Abraham, Isaac and Jacob and all the prophets in the kingdom of God, but you yourselves thrown out. People will come from east and west and north and south, and will take their places at the feast in the kingdom of God.'[1]

This is a story that Luke records Jesus as telling on his way to Jerusalem, which we later read is to be where he is executed. On his way through the villages and towns he is asked a question. Someone asks, 'Lord, are only a few people going to be saved?' You see, as he travelled among the Jews, Jesus was living among people who knew that humans needed to be saved. The question that is asked of Jesus is about how many. Put bluntly, 'How many will escape hell?' Perhaps it's a question that you've wondered about. How many of us will get to heaven? It's a pretty crucial question, isn't it?

Typically, Jesus doesn't reply in the way that we might expect. He doesn't say, 'Not many', or 'Quite a lot actually.' Look at how he replies instead: 'Make every effort to enter through the narrow door, because many, I tell you, will try to enter and will not be able to.'

It's clever, isn't it? Do you see what Jesus does here? He's asked a factual question, the sort that a lot of us like to ask about religion. It's a rather detached and academic question. 'Will a few be saved?' And Jesus replies in the most personal terms imaginable. 'Will you be saved?' Effectively he says, 'Don't worry about the arithmetic of the thing, just make sure you're there.'

Of all the things that Jesus might say to you, I think that this is perhaps the one thing that he'd be keen to impress upon you. You can philosophize endlessly about religion and Jesus and the meaning of the world. But it isn't worth a fig unless you actually do something about it.

Jesus warns you to make every effort. The Greek that this account is written in, speaking of the effort involved here, uses a word that comes from competing in the Games – give it your everything. You don't spend four arduous years qualifying for the Olympics and then walk along behind the other sprinters in your heat. You give it everything; you compete to the utmost of your ability. We already know, from looking at what Jesus would say to Billy Graham, that you won't get in through the door through any effort of your own. You can't earn your way into heaven. In fact it's more difficult than that. You have to strive instead and overcome your pride. Admit that you have made a mess of it, and that there's nothing that you can do to put it right. Humiliating though it is for most people, you have to ask God for his help. It's a narrow door. Not all roads lead to God. Strive to enter through it. Don't kid yourself that you're doing OK and don't need saving.

You need to strive because there are a lot of people

who will try to enter through the narrow door and will not be able to. Jesus goes on to explain why: 'Once the owner of the house gets up and closes the door, you will stand outside knocking and pleading, "Sir, open the door for us." But he will answer, "I don't know you or where you come from."'

The door isn't going to be open for ever. At the moment, says Jesus, you can be saved. If that wasn't the case, why would Jesus be warning them to get on with it? But it isn't going to be like that for ever. Get in there before it's too late. Or miss the feast.

Once the door closes it'll be too late. You can knock and plead, but you'll be turned away. The owner of the house will ask, 'Who are you?' 'Where are you from?' And Jesus says it'll be no good saying, 'We ate and drank with you, and you taught in our streets.' You aren't going to be able to talk your way in.

These are chilling words. It isn't enough to be associated with Jesus. We can be in church, we can eat bread and drink wine and take communion together. We can marvel at his teaching as we read it. But there's only one way to get through the narrow door. That's to respond to Jesus. You have to *do* something about it.

In another story from Luke's biography, Jesus makes this clear:

> 'Why do you call me, "Lord, Lord," and do not do what I say? I will show you what he is like who comes to me and hears my words and puts them into practice. He is like a man

building a house, who dug down deep and laid the foundation on rock. When the flood came, the torrent struck that house but could not shake it, because it was well built. But the one who hears my words and does not put them into practice is like a man who built a house on the ground without a foundation. The moment the torrent struck that house, it collapsed and its destruction was complete.'[2]

It's no use just listening to the words of Jesus. You have to act on them. Unless you do something about this and respond to Jesus you won't be saved. There's no middle ground here. When the door closes, you're either in or you're out.

The consequences of being outside, unable to get to the feast, are catastrophic. 'There will be weeping there, and gnashing of teeth.' There will be great grief and distress. People outside the feast will be completely distraught. Some will gnash their teeth in anger as they rage against God. They'll think it outrageous that God has rejected them – despite perhaps only paying him lip-service (at best) all their lives.

There will be tears of agony, howls of rage, because many are denied access through the shut narrow door. It's hard to imagine a worse scenario. But it does get worse. For two reasons. First, in this door there seems to be a window of some sort. And through that window the Jews who hear this story will see the heroes of the Old Testament: Abraham, Isaac, Jacob and all the prophets. This is a huge jolt for the Jews. This story that Jesus tells them means that being born a Jew isn't enough.

This was the first shock for the Jews, because although there was some debate about it, the general consensus was that all Jews, other than notorious sinners and heretics, would be saved by God. They'd get to heaven. In other words, if you weren't someone who was really extremely evil, you'd be OK.

Isn't that what most people in 'Christian countries' think? 'So long as I live a broadly good life, I'll get to heaven.' It's compulsory heaven for all except Hitler and Saddam Hussein, isn't it? The shock that Jesus has for the Jews is that being a Jew isn't enough. In the same way, for us, being born into what is still sometimes thought of as a Christian country isn't enough. Being a good person and living a reasonable life aren't enough.

Although it's the Jews who are told this story, and are urged to enter through the narrow door, the story is just as relevant to us if we are not Jews. That's why I think Jesus would give you this warning, regardless of your race.

Because the second shock for the Jews is that the places that they thought were going to be theirs are taken by Gentiles – non-Jews from all four points on the compass. Some of those the Jews regarded as last in the pecking order will turn out to be first. And far from being God's first choice by virtue of their being from good religious stock, many of the Jews will be prevented from entering.

The feast is one that we are all invited to. But we have to strive to get there. We can only begin to imagine the agony of those excluded from the feast.

And it could all have been so very different if each one had responded to Jesus. Because there is no other way through the door. Jesus isn't just a spoke in the wheel, not just one option on the way to God. He's the only way to gain entrance to this feast; he is the narrow door.

The fact that this story is addressed to all humankind, both Jews and Gentiles, is only one reason why I think Jesus would remind you of this story. It's also because most of us don't tend to think of our response to him as being in any way urgent. 'Apathy' wouldn't be too strong a term for it. We often put off today what we might get around to tomorrow. Our motto for life might be like that of a group of contemplative nuns, 'Don't just do something, sit there.'

But I think Jesus would want to inject a sense of urgency about this business of entering through the narrow door. That certainly seems to be the reason for his telling the story in the first place. Endless procrastination, putting things off the whole time, is a dangerous game to play.

Especially when that decision is a crucial one. We've all seen the films, haven't we, where the man trying to defuse the bomb is working against the clock? You see it ticking away, counting down the seconds. The guy is snipping away at different coloured wires according to a strict sequence. And do you notice how he always gets to the last two wires and then he can't remember which is the last one? Is it the red or the black? (You do wonder about the quality of training these guys receive – none of them can ever remember.) There are beads of perspiration on his forehead, the clock counts down, the tension mounts, and in the nick of time, with one or two seconds left, he cuts the red wire. And the clock stops. And he's made the right decision – just in time.

This is a decision that is every bit as crucial.

Some of us are looking forward to a deathbed conversion. We figure that we'll live our lives to the full for now and we'll repent at our leisure. Preferably with our last breath. That way we can finally confess to God that we haven't lived how we should, but in the meantime we can go ahead living that way anyway. That's what it boils down to, isn't it?

There's rather a big snag with this, though.

Because all the time the clock is ticking away, counting down the seconds that we have on earth. We were especially aware of time passing in the countdown to the millennium. Millennium clocks showed us how many seconds were left of 1999. The trouble is, unlike these clocks, we have no idea how much time we have left. None of us knows how long the door will be open for. How long do we have to live?

Death is the last great taboo in our society, isn't it? We'll talk about sex till the cows come home, but death? Certainly not in polite society. We'd rather not think about it. Although the idea doesn't bear a moment's examination, we'd rather act as if we were immortal. But we will die. And none of us knows when. We want to put off thinking about it, though, don't we?

Jesus warns us all through this story, 'Don't think you can put off this decision.' If a deathbed conversion is a strategy that appeals to you, you're risking everything on having the luxury of a deathbed. Without it you'll be outside the narrow door, weeping and gnashing your teeth with the rest of them.

And you're also banking on Jesus not coming back first. Jesus told his followers that he'd be returning to the earth one day to wind things up. The end of the world has attracted a great deal of speculation in the last couple of years, with books such as Michael Drosnin's *The Bible Code*, which tried among other things to work out when the world would end. Would it be 2000 or 2006? Films such as *Armageddon* and *Deep Impact* addressed how we might save the world from destruction, and there was brief renewed interest in the predictions of Nostradamus. Jesus' return is something that you may have just written off as the ranting of odd sects. But it's there as one of the central beliefs in orthodox Christianity.

It's not worth spending time trying to speculate how and when it'll happen. In fact, so far as the time is concerned Jesus told his disciples that no-one knows. Not even he did. 'No-one knows about that day or hour, not even the angels in heaven, nor the Son, but only the Father.'[3]

But far from being an excuse for complacency, Jesus went on to say that the very uncertainty of the matter should be a spur to us to be constantly ready:

> 'Be on guard! Be alert! You do not know when that time will come. It's like a man going away: He leaves his house and puts his servants in charge, each with his assigned task, and tells the one at the door to keep watch.
>
> 'Therefore keep watch because you do not know when the owner of the house will come back – whether in the evening, or at midnight, or when the cock crows, or at dawn. If he comes suddenly, do not let him find you sleeping. What I say to you, I say to everyone: "Watch!"'[4]

Jesus makes it clear that his return isn't a matter for endless speculation. No sect is going to hasten his return through their actions. It'll happen, but we don't know when. Again, none of us know how much time is left on the clock. Which is exactly why Jesus warns us to strive to enter the narrow door while we still can.

Faced with defusing a bomb, with the seconds ticking away, you need to take decisive action. If you sit there wondering about it, the thing'll go up in your face. It's the same with this business of accepting or rejecting God. If you leave it too late and don't do something about it, you've had it.

You have the opportunity to get to know God. You must make a decision. Don't put off today what you may not be able to do tomorrow.

Notes

1. What would Jesus say to Oasis?

1. Oasisinet.
2. Oasisinet.
3. *Brothers: From Childhood to Oasis, The Real Story*, by Paul Gallagher and Terry Christian (Virgin Books, 1997), p. 204.
4. Ibid., p. 245.
5. Ibid., p. ix.
6. *Take Me There – Oasis the Story*, by Paul Mathur (Bloomsbury Publishing, 1997), p. 11.
7. *GQ*, February 1998.
8. John 3:1–3.
9. *Oasis Right Here, Right Now*, BBC1.
10. See Luke 15:11–31.
11. Luke 15:13.
12. John 10:10.
13. *Brothers*, p. 72.
14. BBC documentary.

2. What would Jesus say to Prince Charles?

1. *The Prince of Wales, A Biography*, by Jonathan Dimbleby (Little, Brown and Co., 1994), p. 37.
2. Ibid., p. 169.
3. Ibid., p. 225.
4. Speech to Investcorp dinner, 10 July 1996 (copyright St James's Palace and the Press Association Ltd, 1999).
5. Speech to The Prayer Book Society, 29 April 1997 (copyright St James's Palace and the Press Association Ltd, 1999).
6. *The Prince of Wales*, p. 71.
7. Ibid., p. 114.
8. Matthew 7:7–8.
9. Speech 'A sense of the sacred', The Wilton Park Seminar, 13 December 1996 (copyright St James's Palace and the Press Association Ltd, 1999).
10. Ibid., p. 225.
11. Ibid., p. 527.
12. 'Thought for the Day', BBC Radio 4, 8 May 1995 (copyright St James's Palace and the Press Association Ltd, 1999).
13. Speech 'A sense of the sacred'.
14. *Charles: The Private Man, the Public Role*, ITV, June 1994.
15. Speech, King Hussein's memorial service, 5 July 1999 (copyright St James's Palace and the Press Association Ltd, 1999).
16. John 4:9.
17. John 4:11.
18. John 4:13–15.
19. John 4:16–18.
20. John 4:19.
21. John 4:20–24.

3. What would Jesus say to Bridget Jones?

1. *Bridget Jones's Diary*, by Helen Fielding (Picador, 1996), back cover.
2. Ibid.
3. Exodus 20:4–5.

4. *Bridget Jones's Diary*, p. 246.
5. Ibid., p. 105.
6. Ibid., p. 31.
7. Ibid., p. 107.
8. Nehemiah 9:17.
9. Psalm 13:5.
10. Psalm 119:76.
11. Psalm 86:5.
12. Genesis 2:24.
13. Exodus 20:14.
14. *Bridget Jones's Diary*, p. 193.
15. Ibid., p. 310.
16. The full list is in Exodus 20:1–17.
17. Exodus 20:3.
18. Matthew 22:37.

4. What would Jesus say to George Michael?

1. Interview with *Q* magazine, December 1998.
2. Matthew 5:27.
3. Matthew 5:28.
4. Matthew 23:27.
5. John 8:6–11, *The Message*.
6. Interview with *Q* magazine, December 1998.
7. The incident is recorded in 2 Samuel 11.
8. 1 Samuel 21:4–5.
9. 2 Samuel 12:13.
10. Psalm 51:1–4.
11. CNN quotations from Jim Morret's CNN *News Exclusive* interview, 10 April 1998.
12. Psalm 32:1–2, 5.

5. What would Jesus say to Geri Halliwell?

1. Dotmusic – Geri Halliwell (copyright Miller Freeman Entertainment, 1999).
2. Ibid.
3. *The Times*, 6 May 1999.

4. Matthew 11:28–30.
5. *Geri*, a film by Molly Dineen, an RTO Picture for Channel 4, 1999.
6. Ibid.
7. Philippians 4:11–12.
8. *New Britain on the Couch*, by Oliver James, BBC Television series, 1999.
9. *The Times*, 6 May 1999.
10. Philippians 4:13.
11. *The Times*, 6 May 1999.
12. Ibid.
13. Ibid.

6. What would Jesus say to Richard Branson?

1. 'ASAP Interview: Richard Branson', by David Sheff, 24 February 1997 (copyright Forbes 1997).
2. Luke 12:19–20.
3. *Losing my Virginity, The Autobiography*, by Richard Branson (Virgin Publishing, 1998), p. 290.
4. Matthew 19:16.
5. Isaiah 64:6.
6. Matthew 5:28.
7. Matthew 19:21–22.
8. Matthew 19:24.
9. Matthew 19:25.
10. Matthew 19:26.
11. John 17:3.
12. See John 10:10.
13. Matthew 13:44–45.

7. What would Jesus say to Steven Spielberg?

1. 'Steven Spielberg: The Storyteller', by Ronald Grover, *Business Week* magazine, 13 July 1998.
2. Ibid.
3. Ibid.
4. 'Time 100': 'The Moviemaker, Steven Spielberg', by Robert Ebert, in *Time* magazine, 1985.

5. John 8:12.
6. Psalm 119:105.
7. Genesis 1 records God creating the world and consistently reflecting that what he had made was good.
8. Romans 6:23.
9. Revelation 21:4.

8. What would Jesus say to Glenn Hoddle?

1. *The Mirror*, 2 February 1999.
2. *Four Four Two*, February 1995.
3. Interview broadcast on 17 May 1998 on BBC Five Live.
4. John 3:2–3.
5. Interview broadcast on BBC Five Live.
6. *The Times*, 30 January 1999.
7. *Glenn Hoddle – My 1998 World Cup Story*, by Glenn Hoddle with David Davies (André Deutsch, 1998), p. 232.
8. *The Sunday Telegraph*, 31 January 1999.
9. Genesis 3:19.
10. Hebrews 9:27–28.
11. *Glenn Hoddle*, p. 17.
12. Ibid., p. 125.
13. Matthew 6:9–13.
14. *Glenn Hoddle*, p. 54.
15. Expressed in Five Live interview, 17 May 1998.
16. John 1:34.
17. John 5:17–18.
18. John 10:30.
19. John 10:32–33.
20. John 19:7.
21. John 12:44–45.
22. John 14:6–7.
23. John 14:9.
24. John 3:36.

9. What would Jesus say to Mulder and Scully?

1. Episode: *Redux*.
2. John 14:16.
3. Episode: *Talitha Cumi*.
4. Matthew 28:12–13.
5. John 19:33–34.
6. 1 Corinthians 15:6.
7. John 20:25.
8. John 20:26–28.
9. Episode: *Redux*.

10. What would Jesus say to Ben Elton?

1. Genesis 3:1–7.
2. *Popcorn*, by Ben Elton (Pocket Books, 1997), pp. 82–83.
3. Ibid., p. 39.
4. Luke 18:10, *The Message*.
5. Luke 18:11–12, *The Message*.
6. Luke 18:13, *The Message*.
7. Luke 18:14, *The Message*.

11. What would Jesus say to Billy Graham?

1. *Just As I Am*, by Billy Graham (HarperCollins, 1997), p. 24.
2. Ibid., p. 25.
3. Ibid., p. 32.
4. *Billy Graham in Conversation*, by David Frost (Lion, 1997), p. 53.
5. Ibid., p. 57.
6. Matthew 17:21–23.
7. Matthew 7:16.
8. *Just As I Am*, back flap.
9. Ibid., p. 314.
10. Ibid., p. 128.
11. *Billy Graham in Conversation*, p. 112.
12. Ibid., p. 165.
13. *Just As I Am*, p. 727.

14. Ibid., pp. 727, 728.
15. Ibid., p. 728.

12. What would Jesus say to you?

1. Luke 13:22–30.
2. Luke 6:46–49.
3. Mark 13:32.
4. Mark 13:33–37.